HUMAN RIGHTS

A MODERN AGENDA

HUMAN RIGHTS

A MODERN AGENDA

Edited by

Alan Miller

Visiting Professor of Law, University of Strathclyde

T&T CLARK
EDINBURGH
2000

T&T CLARK LTD
59 GEORGE STREET
EDINBURGH EH2 2LQ
SCOTLAND

Copyright © T&T Clark and the authors, 2000

All rights reserved. No part of this publication may be reproduced, stored in a retrieval system, or transmitted, in any form or by any means, electronic, mechanical, photocopying, recording or otherwise, without the prior permission of T&T Clark Ltd.

First published 2000

ISBN 0 567 00540 2

British Library Cataloguing-in-Publication Data
A catalogue record for this book is available from the British Library

Typeset by Fakenham Photosetting Ltd, Fakenham, Norfolk
Printed and bound by MPG Books, Bodmin

CONTENTS

Table of Cases vii

Table of Statutes xiii

Table of International Instruments xv

The Authors 1

Introduction 3

1. A Modern Human Rights Agenda
   Alan Miller 7

2. International Human Rights in a Devolved Scotland
   Rebecca M M Wallace and Kenneth Dale-Risk 23

3. The Scottish Parliament and the Rights of the Child
   Kathleen Marshall 37

4. Incorporation and Interpretation of Guarantees for Respect for Private Life: A Threat to Press Freedom?
   Jim Murdoch 51

5. Opening up Government: Paradise Postponed Again?
   Mark Poustie 67

6. Scottish Criminal Justice and the Human Rights Act
   Christopher Gane 97

7. Criminal Procedure, Convention Rights and the Consequences of Incorporation
   Alastair Brown 117

TABLE OF CASES

A v United Kingdom, ECHR, 23 September 1998; 5 BHRC 137 40
A-G v Guardian Newspapers (No 2) [1990] 1 AC 109 52
Adair v McGarry 1933 JC 72; 1933 SLT 482 127
Adamson v Martin 1916 SC 319. 55
Advocate (H M) v Boyle 1993 JC 5; 1993 SLT 1079; 1992 SCCR 939 112
— v K 1994 SCCR 499 108
— v Little 1999 SCCR 625 118
— v McGlinchey and Renicks 18 February 2000 133
— v Martin and Others 1956 JC 1; 1956 SLT 193 110
— v O'Neill 1992 SLT 303; 1992 SCCR 130 112
— v Scottish Media Newspapers Ltd 1999 SCCR 599 118
— v Wilson 1984 SLT 117; 1983 SCCR 420 110
Advocate (Lord) v Scotsman Publications Ltd 1989 SLT 705; [1989] 1 AC 812   72
Airey v Ireland (1979–80) 2 EHRR 305 . . . . 61, 63
Aldred v Miller 1925 JC 21 60
Anderson v H M Advocate 1998 SLT 155 . . . . 120, 122–124
Asch v Austria (1993) 15 EHRR 597 131
Attorney General v Guardian Newspapers Ltd (No 2) [1990] 1 AC 109 . 52, 68, 72
Attorney-General for Canada v Attorney-General for Ontario [1937] AC 326 25

Barbera, Messegue and Jabardo v Spain (1989) 11 EHRR 360 129
Barty v Hill 1907 SC (J) 36, (1907) 14 SLT 616 110
Belgian Linguistics case (1968) 1 EHRR 252 58
Bennett, Petitioner 1995 SLT 510; 1994 SCCR 902 112
Bett v Hamilton 1997 SLT 1310; 1997 SCCR 621 110
Black v Carmichael, Carmichael v Black 1992 SLT 897 99
Boner v UK (1995) 19 EHRR 246 52
Bott v Anderson 1995 JC 178; 1995 SLT 1308; 1995 SCCR 584 112
Boyle v H M Advocate 1976 JC 32; 1976 SLT 126 . . . . 110, 111
Brogan v United Kingdom (1989) 11 EHRR 117 126
Brüggemann and Scheuten v Germany, DR 10, 100 59

CC v United Kingdom [1999] Crim LR 228 126
CR v United Kingdom (1995) 21 EHRR 363 . . . . 101, 102
Cameron v Normand 1992 SCCR 866 107
Campbell and Cosans v United Kingdom (1982) 4 EHRR 293 . . . . . 39, 40, 52
Carmichael v Ashrif 1985 SCCR 461 108
Carvel v Council of the European Union (t-194/94) [1996] All ER (EC) 53, [1995] 3 CMLR 359 97
Castells v Spain (sub nom Castes v Spain) (1992) 14 EHRR 445 64
Chappell v UK, 30 Mar 1989, Ser A No 152-A 61
Chinoy v United Kingdom, Application No 15199/89, 4 September 1991 . . . 125
Christie v United Kingdom (1994) 78-A DR 119 72
Coats (J & P) Ltd v Brown 1909 SC (J) 29, (1909) 6 Adam 19 . . . . . . 112, 113
Colhoun v Friel 1996 SLT 1252, 1996 SCCR 497 107

Costello-Roberts v UK (1995) 19 EHRR 112 58
Currie v McGlennan 1989 SLT 872 127

Dean v John Menzies (Holdings) Ltd 1981 JC 23; 1981 SLT 50 108
Derbyshire County Council v Times Newspapers Ltd [1993] 1 All ER 1011 (HL) 54
Dombo Beheer BV v Netherlands (1994) 18 EHRR 213] 127
Donaldson v Vannet 1998 SLT 957; 1998 SCCR 421 107
Donnelly v H M Advocate 1984 SCCR 93 112
Doorson v The Netherlands (1996) 22 EHRR 330 . . . . 128, 129
Dubowska and Skup v Poland, European Commission on Human Rights . . 115
Dudgeon v UK (1981) 4 EHRR 149 . . . . 58, 60–62, 64, 65, 114
Duffield v Skeen 1981 SCCR 66 107

Edwards v United Kingdom (1993) 15 EHRR 417 123
Exchange of Greek and Turkish Populations Case PCIJ Rep, Ser B, No 10, p 20 (1925) 25

Fisher v Keane 1981 SLT (Notes) 28 105
Foster v British Gas C-188/89 [1991] 2 AC 306 80
Friedl v Austria (1996) 21 EHRR 83 58
Friel v Initial Contract Services Ltd 1994 SLT 1216, 1993 SCCR 675 110
Funke v France (1993) 16 EHRR 297 124

G v France, European Court of Human Rights, 29/1994/47/6/557 (1995) . . 101
Gaskin v United Kingdom (1990) 12 EHRR 36 70
Granger v UK, 28 Mar 1990, Ser A No 174, [1990] TLR 256 52
Grant v Allan 1987 JC 71; 1988 SLT 11; 1987 SCCR 402 105
Gray (John) (1737) Hume, i, 441 103
Greenhuff (Bernard) (1838) 2 Swinton 236 103–105
Griffin v South West Water Services [1995] IRLR 15 80
Groppera Radio AG and Others v Switzerland (1990)13 EHRR 321 101
Guerra v Italy (1988) 26 EHRR 357 70

Handyside v United Kingdom (1976) 1 EHRR 737 . . . . 62, 63
Hellewell v Chief Constable of Derbyshire [1995] 1 WLR 804 . . . . 54, 55
Henderson v Chief Constable, Fife Police 1988 SLT 361 55
Herron v Best 1976 SLT (Sh Ct) 80 99
Hewitt and Harman v United Kingdom (1992) 14 EHRR 657 71
Horsburgh v Russell 1994 SLT 942, 1994 SCCR 237 108
Hutcheson v United Kingdom [1997] EHRLR 195 58

Ingram v Macari 1983 SLT 61, 1982 SCCR 372 108

Jardine v Crowe 1999 JC 59, 1999 SCCR 52 120
Johnston v Ireland, 18 Dec 1986, Ser A No 112 61

Kaur v Lord Advocate 1980 SC 319; 1981 SLT 322 . . . . 8, 27, 53
Kemmache No 1 v France (1992) 14 EHRR 520 126

Kerr v Hill 1936 JC 71; 1936 SLT 320 . . . . 104, 106
Khaliq v H M Advocate 1984 JC 23; 1984 SLT 137; 1983 SCCR 483 . 104, 108, 109
Klass v Germany (1978) 2 EHRR 214 . . . . 57, 58, 60, 62, 72
Kokkinakis v Greece, European Court of Human Rights, Ser A, No 260-A 101, 102
Kopp v Switzerland (1999) 27 EHRR 91 101
Kroon v Netherlands (1995) 19 EHRR 263 61

Lamy v Belgium (1989) 11 EHRR 529 127
Laskey, Jaggard and Brown v United Kingdom, 19 Feb 1997, RJD 1997-I . . . 59
Latto v Vannet 1997 SCCR 721 112
Law Hospital NHS Trust v Lord Advocate 1996 SC 30;, 1996 SLT 848 113
Lawrie v Muir 1950 JC 19; 1950 SLT 37 125
Leander v Sweden (1987) 9 EHRR 433 . . . . 60, 70
Letellier v France (1992) 14 EHRR 83 . . . . 126, 127
Lingens v Austria (1986) 8 EHRR 407 . . . . 58, 59, 63, 64
Lithgow v UK, Ser A No 102 62
Lockhart v Stephen 1987 SCR 642 (Sh Ct) 108

McBain v Crichton 1961 JC 25; 1961 SLT 209 113
MacCormick v Lord Advocate 1953 SC 396 16
McDougall v Dochree 1992 JC 154; 1992 SLT 624; 1992 SCCR 531 107
McFadyen v Annan 1992 JC 53; 1992 SLT 163; 1992 SCCR 186 112
Mackenzie v H M Advocate 1969 JC 52; 1970 SLT 81 110
McKenzie v Normand 1992 SLT 130; 1992 SCCR 14 107
McLaughlan v Boyd 1936 JC 71; 1936 SLT 320 . . . . 106, 108
MacLean (John), *The Scotsman*, 30 October 1979 107
McLeod (Alastair) v HM Advocate 1998 JC 67; 1998 SLT 233; 1998 SCCR 77 (*sub nom* McLeod, Petitioner) 8, 120, 122–124
McMichael v United Kingdom [1995] 2 FCR 718; (1995) 20 EHRR 205 . 40, 41, 52
Maile v Wigan Metropolitan Borough Council [1999] 294 ENDS Report 55 . 81
Malone v Metropolitan Police Commissioner (No 2) [1979] Ch 344 60
Malone v UK (1984) 7 EHRR 14 . . . . 61, 71
Marckx v Belgium (1979) 2 EHRR 330 60
Matznetter v Austria (1979–80) 1 EHRR 198 126
Maxwell v UK (1995) 19 EHRR 97 52
Mecklenburg v Kreis Pinneberg C-321/96 [1998] 10 ELM 252 . . . . 79, 81
Meehan v Inglis 1975 JC 9; 1974 SLT (Notes) 61 113
Meekison (John) and Tutor v Mackay (1848) Arkley 503 107
Miln v Cullen 1967 JC 21; 1967 SLT 35 . . . . 128, 129
Montgomery v McLeod 1977 SLT (Notes) 77; (1977) SCCR Supplement 164 . 107
Montgomery and Coulter v H M Advocate 16 November 1999 133
Moore v Secretary of State for Scotland 1985 SLT 38 53
Mowbray v Crowe 1993 JC 212; 1994 SLT 445; 1993 SCCR 730 112
Müller v Switzerland, 24 May 1988, Ser A No 133 63
Murray v United Kingdom (1996) 22 EHRR 29 130

N v Portugal, Application no 20683/92 (unreported) 62
Niemietz v Germany (1993) 16 EHRR 97 . . . . 58, 59, 64

Norris v Ireland (1988) 13 EHRR 245 114

Olsson v Sweden (No 2) (1994) 17 EHRR 134 64
Osman v United Kingdom (2000) 29 EHRR 245 115
Otto-Preminger Institute v Austria (1995) 19 EHRR 34 63

Powell & Rayner v UK, 21 Feb 1990, Ser A No 172, [1990] TLR 142 58
Prager and Öberschlick v Austria (1996) 21 EHRR 1 64

R v British Coal Corporation, ex parte Ibstock Building Products Ltd [1995] Env LR 277 . . . . 79, 81
R v General Council of the Bar, ex parte Percival [1991] 1 QB 212; [1990] 3 WLR 323;
[1990] 3 All ER 137 113
R v H M Advocate 1988 SLT 623; 1988 SCCR 254 108
R v Inland Revenue Commissioners, ex parte Mead [1993] 1 All ER 772 . . . 113
R v Ponting [1985] Crim LR 318 72
R v Rochdale Metropolitan Borough Council, ex parte Brown [1997] Env LR 100
  73
R v Secretary of State for the Home Department, ex parte Brind [1991] 1 AC 696
  8, 119, 120
Raffaelli v Heatly 1949 JC 101; 1949 SLT 284 107
Rees v UK [1987] 2 FLR 111 . . . . 58, 62
Robertson v Smith 1980 JC 1; 1979 SLT (Notes) 51 108

SW v United Kingdom (1995) 21 EHRR 363 . . . . 100, 101
Salabiaku v France (1991) 13 EHRR 379 130
Salomon v Commissioners of Customs and Excise [1967] 2 QB 116 27
Saunders v United Kingdom (1997) 23 EHRR 3131 130
Schenk v Switzerland (1991) 13 EHRR 242 125
Scott v Smith 1981 JC 46; 1981 SLT (Notes) 22 108
Sheffield and Horsham v United Kingdom, 30 July 1998, RJD 1998-V 2011 . . 59
Sinclair v Annan 1980 SLT (Notes) 55 107
Skeen v McLaren 1976 SLT (Notes) 14 129
Smith v McCallum 1982 SLT 421; 1982 SCCR 115 127
Soering v United Kingdom (1989) 11 EHRR 439 . . . . 128, 129
Spencer (Earl) and Countess Spencer v United Kingdom (Application Nos 28851/95 and 28852/95) decision of 16 Jan 1998, 25 EHRR CD 105 . . . 54, 57
Starrs v Ruxton: Ruxton v Starrs 2000 SLT 42; 1999 SCCR 1052 . . . . 3, 133
Steel and Others v United Kingdom (1999) 28 EHRR 603 108
Stewart v Lockhart 1990 SCCR 390 107
Stewart-Brady v United Kingdom, Application nos 27436/95 and 28406/95, 2 July 1997 (unreported) 62
Stirrat v City of Edinburgh Council 1998 SCLR 971; [1998] 10 ELM 220 73
Stirrat Park Hogg v Dumbarton District Council 1996 SLT 1113; 1994 SCLR 631
  77, 78
Stjerna v Finland (1997) 24 EHRR 195 58
Strathern v Seaforth 1926 JC 100; 1926 SLT 445 . . . . 104, 106
Stuurman v H M Advocate 1980 JC 111; 1980 SLT (Notes) 95 112

Sugden v H M Advocate 1934 JC 103 104
Sunday Times v UK (1979–80) 2 EHRR 245 . . . . 61, 101

T, Petitioner 1997 SLT 724; 1996 SCLR 897 . . . . 8, 27, 53, 119, 123
T v United Kingdom, European Commission on Human Rights, Application No
    24724/94 114
Taylor v Hamilton 1984 SCCR 393 107
Taylor and Others, 19 October 1808, Burnett, *A Treatise on Various Branches of the
    Criminal Law of Scotland*, 1811, Appendix X 103
Thompson v MacPhail 1989 SLT 637; 1989 SCCR 266 107
Tomasi v France (1993) 15 EHRR 1 . . . . 126, 127
Torres v H M Advocate 1997 SCCR 491 112
Toth v Austria (1992) 14 EHRR 551 126
Trapp v M, Trapp v Y 1971 SLT (Notes) 30 113
Tudhope v Barlow 1981 SLT (Sh Ct) 94 108
Turner v Kennedy (1972) SCCR Supplement 30 103
Tyrer v United Kingdom [1978] 2 EHRR 1 25

Ucak v H M Advocate 1998 SCCR 517 123
Unterpertinger v Austria (1991) 13 EHRR 175 131

V v United Kingdom [2000] 2 All ER 1024 (Note); 2000 Crim LR 187 114

WWF UK v EC Commission (T-105/95) [1997] All ER (EC) 300, ECR II-313, [1997]
    9 ELM 113 . . . . 96, 97
Watt v Annan 1978 JC 84, 1978 SLT 198 . . . . 106, 108
Winterwerp v Netherlands (1979–80) 2 EHRR 387 125
Woolmington v DPP [1935] AC 462 . . . . 129, 130
Wordie Property Co Ltd v Secretary of State for Scotland 1984 SLT 345 . . . 81
Wyness v Lockhart 1992 SCCR 808 107

X v Sweeney 1982 JC 70; 1983 SLT 48; 1982 SCCR 161 . . . . 59, 112, 113
X & Y v Netherlands, 26 Mar 1985, Ser A No 91 . . . . 58, 114

Young v Heatly 1959 JC 66; 1959 SLT 250 107

Z v Austria No. 10392/83 56 DR 13 (1988) 70

TABLE OF STATUTES

1707	Act of Union 11		s 7 71
1887	Criminal Procedure (Scotland) Act (50 & 51 Vict. c. 35) . 100		s 8 71
		1987	Access to Personal Files Act (c. 37) 68, 73
1911	Official Secrets Act (1 & 2 Geo. 5, c. 28)		s 1 74
	s 2 . . . . 69, 72	1988	Access to Medical Reports Act (c. 28) 68, 75
1958	Public Records Act (6 & 7 Eliz. 2, c. 51) 87	1989	Security Service Act (c. 5) . . . 71
			s 1(2)–(4) 71
1961	Rivers (Prevention of Pollution) Act (9 & 10 Eliz. 2, c. 50)		s 4 71
			s 5 71
	s 12 76		Official Secrets Act (c. 6) . 69, 72
1967	Public Records Act (c. 44) . . 87		s 1 72
1969	Genocide Act (c. 12) 26	1990	Access to Health Records Act (c. 23) 75
1970	Equal Pay Act (c. 41) 13		
1973	Local Government (Scotland) Act (c. 65) 68		Human Fertilisation and Embryology Act (c. 37) . 75
	ss 38–49 73		Environmental Protection Act (c. 43) 88
	ss 50A–B 73		
	s 50B(1) 73		s 20 . . . . 68, 77
	(3) 73		(1) 77
	ss 50C–D 73		(7) 77
	s 50E 73		s 21 78
	s 50H(2)(b) 73		s 22 78
	s 50J 73		s 64 . . . . 68, 77
	s 101(1) 73		s 65 78
	Sched 7A 73		s 66 78
1974	Control of Pollution Act (c. 40) 76		s 78S 78
			s 78T 78
	Pt III 77		s 120 68
	s 41 77	1993	Radioactive Substances Act (c. 12)
	s 42A 78		
	s 42B 78		s 39 . . . . 77, 78
1975	Sex Discrimination Act (c. 65) 13	1994	Intelligence Services Act (c. 13) 71
1976	Race Relations Act (c. 74) 13, 26		s 1 71
			s 3 71
1984	Data Protection Act (c. 35) 68, 73, 74		s 8 71
			s 9 71
1985	Companies Act (c. 6) 68		s 10 71
	Local Government (Access to Information) Act (c. 43) 68, 69, 73	1995	Children (Scotland) Act (c. 36) 38
			Criminal Law (Consolidation) (Scotland) Act (c. 39) . 121
	Food and Environment Protection Act (c. 48) . . 77		Proceeds of Crime (Scotland) Act (c. 43) 121, 122
	Interception of Communications Act (c. 56)		

	Criminal Procedure (Scotland) Act (c. 46) 121	(b) 117
	s 14 126	(3) 9, 56
	s 259 130	s 7 115
	Sched 3, para 2 100	(1) 114
	Disability Discrimination Act (c. 50) 13	(7) 113
		s 8 9
1996	Security Service Act (c. 35) . 71	(1) 9
	Broadcasting Act (c. 55)	s 10 . . . . 9, 27, 54
	s 107 55	s 12 . . . . 55, 56
1997	Town and Country Planning (Scotland) Act (c. 8)	s 19 9
		s 21 117
	s 36 77	Scotland Act (c. 46) . . 1, 2, 7, 8, 15, 17, 21, 27, 28, 35, 37, 52, 53, 113, 119, 121
	Planning (Hazardous Substances) (Scotland) Act (c. 10)	
		s 28 54
	s 27 77	s 29 . . . . 7, 23, 27
	Crime and Punishment (Scotland) Act (c. 48) . 122	(1) 11, 23, 24, 122
		(2) 11, 122
1998	Data Protection Act (c. 29) . 68, 73, 75, 88, 92	(d) 23
		s 35 . . . . 12, 23, 24
	Pt II 74	(1) 24
	Pt IV 74	s 44 . . . . 114, 116
	Pt V 74	(1)(c) 116
	s 1(1) 55, 74	s 53(2) 54
	s 2 55	s 57 . . . . 7, 23, 132
	s 6 74	(2) . . 11, 114, 116, 121, 133
	ss 17–21 74	(3) 116, 117, 121
	s 32 55	s 58 . . . . 12, 24
	ss 51–54 74	(1) 24, 31
	Sched 1, Pt I 74	(2) 24
	Human Rights Act (c. 42) . 1–3, 7, 8, 10, 13–15, 21, 27, 28, 47, 49, 52, 53, 62, 63, 68, 70, 97, 118, 119, 121, 124	(4)(a) 24
		s 63 13
		s 102(2) 11
		s 103 14
		s 112 . . . . (1)
	s 2(1) 8, 27	 24
	ss 3–5 54	Sched 5 13
	s 3 121	section L2 13
	(1) 8	para 7(1) 12, 23
	s 4 27	(2) 12, 28
	(2) 8	(a) 23
	(6) 121	Sched 6 114
	ss 6–8 54	1999	Mental Health (Public Safety and Appeals) (Scotland) Act (ASP 1) 3
	s 6(1) 9, 113, 116, 121	
	(2) 116, 117, 121	
	(a) 117	

TABLE OF INTERNATIONAL INSTRUMENTS

Cultural Agreement and Exchange of Letters between Canada and France,
November 1965 32
Declaration of the Rights of the Child 1924 38
Directive 90/313/EEC (OJ [1990] L158/56) 76, 79
    Art 3 81
    Art 4 81
    Art 7 84
Directive 95/46/EC (OJ L281, 24.10.95) 74
Directive 96/61/EC (OJ L257/26, 24.9.96) 79
    Art 15(3) 78
Draft Declaration on the Rights and Duties of States 1949
    Art 13 25
EC Treaty
    Art 226 95
    Art 253 95
European Convention on Human Rights and Fundamental Freedoms 1950 . 1–3,
7–11, 13, 14, 17, 18, 23,
24, 26–28, 32, 33, 35, 37–39, 42, 43,
46, 47, 51–54, 61, 62, 65, 68, 70,
113, 114, 116–122, 132, 133
    Art 1 39
    Art 2 . . . . 115, 125
        (1) 101
    Art 3 . . . . 13, 25, 26, 28, 40, 128
    Art 5 . . . . 124, 125
        (1) 101
            (a)–(e) 125
            (c) 126
        (3) 126, 127
        (4) 127
    Art 6 . . . . 3, 13, 118, 119, 124, 128, 131, 132
        (1) 8, 40, 114, 122, 125, 131
        (2) 129, 130
        (3)(a)–(c) 122
            (b) 123
            (d) 129, 130, 131
    Art 7 . . . . 100, 101, 102
        (1) 102, 105
        (2) 105
    Art 8 . . . . 13, 39, 40, 55, 56–59, 62–64, 70, 114, 124, 125, 127
        (1) 57, 70
        (2) 101, 124
    Art 9 59
        (2) 101
    Art 10 . . . . 55–57, 59, 62–64, 70, 114
        (2) 101

Art 11 . . . . 59, 114
    (2) 101
Art 13 57
Art 26 27
Art 27(2) 27
Art 31 27
Art 46 27
Art 63(3) 26
Protocol 1 125
Protocol 11 26
European Convention for the Prevention of Torture and Inhuman or
    Degrading Treatment or Punishment 1979 28
Geneva Convention Relating to the Status of Refugees 1951 26
International Convention on Elimination of All Forms of Racial Discrimination
    1966 . . . . 18, 28
    Art 1, para 1 30
    Art 5 30
    Art 8 30
International Covenant on Civil and Political Rights 1966 . . . . 12, 18, 25, 28
International Covenant on Economic, Social and Cultural Rights
    1966 . . . . 12, 16, 18, 28
    Art 1.1 . . . . 28, 29
    Art 6.1 29
    Art 7 29
    Art 8 29
    Art 9 29
    Art 11 29
    Art 12 29
    Art 13 . . . . 29, 30
Maastricht Treaty 1992 97
Rio Declaration on Environment and Development, 13 June 1992, UNCED,
    A/Conf/151/4 Principle 10 77
United Nations Charter 1945 39
United Nations Convention Against Torture and Other Cruel, Inhuman or
    Degrading Treatment or Punishment 1984 28
    Art 17 30
    Art 22 30
United Nations Convention on the Elimination of All Forms of Discrimination
    Against Women 1979 . . . . 12, 18, 28
    Art 2(b) 29
    Art 10 30
United Nations Convention on the Prevention and Punishment of the Crime of
    Genocide 1948
    Art II 26
United Nations Convention on the Rights of the Child 1989 . 28, 38, 40–42, 46, 47
    Art 3 43
    Art 9 42
    Art 12 . . . . 43, 45
    Art 19 42

Table of International Instruments xvii

United Nations Convention on the Rights of the Child 1992 . . . . 12, 18, 37
   Art 3 29
United Nations Declaration of the Principles of International Culture
   Co-operation, 4 November 1966 19
United Nations Declaration on the Right of Peoples to Peace, 12 November
   1984 19
United Nations Declaration on the Use of Scientific and Technological Progress
   in the Interests of Peace and for the Benefit of Mankind, 10 November
   1975 19
United Nations Economic Commission for Europe Convention on access to
   information, public participation in decision-making and access to justice
   in environmental matters (the Aarhus Convention) 1998 . . . . 77, 92
United Nations General Assembly Resolution 48/134, 20 December 1993 . . . 33
   Preamble 33
United Nations General Assembly Resolution 59(2), 14 December 1946 67
United Nations Universal Declaration on the Eradication of Hunger and
   Malnutrition, 16 November 1974 19
Universal Declaration of Human Rights 1948 . . . . 19, 28, 38, 39, 43
Vienna Declaration on Human Rights 1993 33

THE AUTHORS

Alastair Brown is a solicitor qualified in both Scots and English law. He is a member of the Procurator Fiscal Service and holds a PhD in the relationship between international law (including human rights law) and criminal law.

Kenneth Dale-Risk has lectured at Napier University since February 1997 having previously practised as a solicitor. He is heavily involved in research into human rights issues and is co-author with Professor Rebecca Wallace of *Companion to the European Convention on Human Rights*.

Christopher Gane is Professor of Scots Law at the University of Aberdeen. He has written extensively on criminal law and human rights and enjoys a deserved international reputation.

Kathleen Marshall is a solicitor, child law consultant and Visiting Professor to the Centre for the Child and Society, University of Glasgow. She was formerly Director of the Scottish Child Law Centre and her consultancy work has dealt with issues such as support for children and families and child protection. She chaired the Edinburgh Inquiry into Abuse and Protection of Children in Care which reported in February 1999 and she has also written and presented numerous papers on aspects of child law and children's rights and is author of *Children's Rights in the Balance: the Participation–Protection Debate*, published by the Stationery Office in 1997.

Alan Miller is an experienced practising lawyer, a partner of the Human Rights Law Consultancy (a division of Lambie Law Partnership) and President of the Glasgow Bar Association. Since 1996 he has been a Visiting Professor of Law, specialising in human rights, at the University of Strathclyde. He is also a member of the Centre for Human Rights Law based at the Glasgow Graduate School of Law. As Director of the Scottish Human Rights Centre he has been invited to present oral submissions to the United Nations in Geneva concerning the application of international human rights treaties within Scotland. He has been a participant in the Scottish Office consultative steering group process through his membership of the Expert Panel on Standing Orders and Working Procedures of the Scottish Parliament and also the Working Group on a Code of Conduct for Members of the Scottish Parliament. He has since been appointed by the Scottish Office to represent Scottish interests in the Home Office task force overseeing preparations for the implementation of the Human Rights Act throughout the United Kingdom. A Scottish member of the Editorial Board of Sweet & Maxwell's *European Human Rights Law Review*, he is also Human Rights Editor of Green's *Scottish Parliament Law Review*.

Jim Murdoch is Professor of Public Law and Head of the School of Law at the University of Glasgow. He is a member of the Centre for Human Rights Law, based at the Glasgow Graduate School of Law which is a joint venture of the University of Strathclyde and the University of Glasgow. He is a frequent contributor to Council of Europe seminar programmes in central and east Europe and has written extensively on European human rights protection.

Mark Poustie is a solicitor and senior lecturer in law at the University of Strathclyde. He teaches human rights law and aspects of public law in addition to planning and environmental law. His publications include *Pollution Control: The Law in Scotland*, T&T Clark, 1997 (with Smith & Collar)—which incorporates a chapter on access to environmental information—and *The Legal System of Scotland—Cases & Materials*, 4th ed, W Green, 1999 (with Paterson & Bates) together with numerous articles on environmental law issues. He is also a member of the Centre for Human Rights Law which is a joint venture of the University of Strathclyde and the University of Glasgow.

Rebecca Wallace has been Head of the Law Department at Napier University since January 1997 and has over twenty years' experience in the teaching of international law, with a particular emphasis on human rights issues. An extensive list of publications includes *International Law: a Student's Text* and *International Human Rights: Text and Materials*. Professor Wallace was Ariel Sallows Professor of Human Rights at the University of Saskatchewan, Canada in 1994 and has been appointed a member of the Advisory Committee at the Centre for Gender and Refugee Studies, Hastings College of Law, University of California. She was called to the English Bar by the academic route in November 1999.

INTRODUCTION

The curtain has now risen on a modern drama for the 21st century. The stage is public life in a changed and changing Scotland. The first act has begun and the scenery has been shifted to prepare for the second act. New characters are appearing, others are anticipated and the audience expects to participate.

The first act features the Scotland Act 1998, which has introduced a Scottish Parliament with significant law-making powers and human rights responsibilities. Its constitutional guarantee to all persons of those rights contained within the European Convention on Human Rights (ECHR) brings forward the character of human rights—its role still to be broadened and fully defined—from the wings to centre stage.

The scenery has been prepared for the second act, the Human Rights Act of 1998, which commenced on 2 October 2000. Public authorities, including courts, tribunals, local government, police and certain 'quangos', now enter stage and are required to comply with those rights contained within the ECHR.

If the Scotland Act and the Human Rights Act are responsible for changing the scenery in Scotland's public life then it is the past century's increasing demand for self-determination—as a nation and as individual citizens—which has been the inspiration for change. The universality of the demand for change has brought an international audience to witness whether this Scottish drama may shed a light beyond Scotland's borders.

The first two acts have whetted the appetite for more. They have raised questions full of significance for Scotland, the United Kingdom and humanity itself, such as what will be the role of human rights in the 21st century? The real intrigue, of course, is that the script for the opening acts, including the ECHR itself, was written last century and it is up to this new century and the audience, at home and abroad, to participate in writing the rest of the script and producing the answers.

'Human Rights: A Modern Agenda' is the first book of its kind to examine the implications of the interface between the Scotland Act and the Human Rights Act. Its purpose is to increase awareness and stimulate public debate about a new role for human rights in a changed and still changing Scotland. It should be of interest to not only the legal and academic communities but also the wider Scottish public and beyond. The book raises critical questions and provides facts as well as opinions to help inform the public debate on the implications of the most profound constitutional and legal change in Scotland for the past three centuries.

What will be the impact of the Scotland Act and the Human Rights Act on the governance of Scotland and of the United Kingdom? What is the potential impact upon the international stage? What is the ECHR and what other international human rights treaties are now the responsibility of the Scottish Parliament? In particular, what will application of the United Nations Convention on the Rights of the Child mean in practice? What developments in privacy law and freedom of information may now be anticipated? How significant will be the impact of the ECHR on Scotland's criminal justice system?

A wide range of significant contributors address these and other relevant questions. Each is respected in his/her own field and brings a combination of academic expertise and practical experience to what should be a seminal publication.

The first chapter is concerned with the development of a modern human rights agenda able to meet the needs of the 21st century. From that perspective I analyse the impact of the Scotland Act and the Human Rights Act on the governance of Scotland, the United Kingdom and upon the international stage. These questions are explored by examining the key provisions of both Acts, how they interface, the human rights responsibilities of the Scottish Parliament and its potential relations in this field with the Westminster Parliament and the international community.

In chapter 2, Rebecca Wallace and Kenneth Dale-Risk consider the obligations incumbent upon the Scottish Parliament to comply with international human rights treaties. The parliament's competence in the observance of international obligations is analysed, and while the importance of the ECHR is recognised, emphasis is placed on other equally significant human rights instruments. The chapter concludes with a discussion of the creation of a human rights culture within the United Kingdom. Particular consideration is given to the development of an appropriate institution for Scotland to support the new parliament and develop a public awareness of human rights throughout the nation. This chapter is very topical given the increasing interest in the establishment by the parliament of a Scottish Human Rights Commission.

In chapter 3, Kathleen Marshall recognises that the Scotland Act and the Human Rights Act have set up a new dynamic with regard to human rights in Scotland. Whilst welcoming this development, many of Scotland's child welfare agencies, and academics working in the children's field, have argued that the picture remains incomplete due to the lack of an equally powerful commitment to the 1989 UN Convention on the Rights of the Child. Professor Marshall explores the relationship between 'children's rights' and 'human rights' and identifies steps which might be taken to ensure that the rights of children are respected in a new Scotland.

Jim Murdoch notes in chapter 4 that the use of the ECHR to challenge Scots law in practice has been comparatively minimal, reflecting the failure of the Scottish courts to exhibit much in the way of sympathy towards attempts to use the Convention as an informal source on legal arguments. Incorporation is thus likely to have an even greater impact on Scotland than elsewhere in the United Kingdom where discussion of the Convention has been more commonplace. However, throughout the United Kingdom, a shared concern has been the potential impact of Article 8 of ECHR requiring respect for private life. Judges, it is suggested, are poised to construct a new law of privacy against media intrusion. This chapter assesses relevant Strasbourg case law with the aim of evaluating possible outcomes in the search for an appropriate balance between individual liberty and press freedom.

In chapter 5, Mark Poustie provides a comprehensive background on the progress towards a new freedom of information regime in the United Kingdom and in Scotland. The UK Freedom of Information Bill is scrutinised, its shortcomings explained and the chapter also anticipates the potential effects of the Human Rights Act and incorporation of the European Convention on Human Rights as well as a proposed Scottish Freedom of Information Bill.

Read together, chapters 6 and 7 reflect the dynamic of the coming debate within Scotland's criminal justice system regarding the interpretation to be placed by the judiciary on the relevance of the ECHR to existing Scottish criminal law and practice.

Introduction

Chris Gane argues in chapter 6 that the effect of the Human Rights Act and the ECHR upon our system of criminal justice is potentially very significant. He concentrates on two salient and central features of our criminal justice system and analyses the extent to which challenges may arise under the Human Rights Act. The first is the much-vaunted 'flexibility' of our criminal law (or, more specifically, the common law) and the second is the very extensive degree of discretion exercised by the public prosecutor in Scotland and the very limited external controls over the exercise of that discretion.

In chapter 7, Alastair Brown accepts that the incorporation of the ECHR will have a significant and welcome effect on criminal law and practice in Scotland. He is concerned with the nature of that effect and argues, under reference to existing case law, the retention of the sovereignty of the Westminster Parliament and a comparison of aspects of ECHR law and Scots criminal procedure law, that it will be organic or evolutionary rather than disjunctive.

The potential impact of the ECHR has already been illustrated in the case of *Starrs v Ruxton; Ruxton v Starrs* 1999 SCCR 1052 which decided that a temporary sheriff, lacking adequate security of tenure, did not constitute an 'independent and impartial tribunal' as required by Art 6, 'right to a fair and public hearing'. From 2 October, 2000, of course, Art 6 applies to a whole range of courts, tribunals and other decision-making bodies and processes and many of these can be expected to be subjected to unprecedented scrutiny and, in many instances, legal challenge.

Similarly, the challenges at Lanark Sheriff Court by two patients in Carstairs State Hospital, Toner and Docherty, against the retrospective effect of the Scottish Parliament's first piece of legislation, namely, the Mental Health (Public Safety & Appeals) (Scotland) Act 1999, served notice on the parliament that it too is not beyond the reach of the ECHR.

We are therefore entering new times full of challenge and placing a responsibility upon us all to begin to place human rights where they belong—no longer at the margins but at the centre of development of society.

I would like to thank the authors for contributing to the debate on these important issues and express our appreciation to the Clark Foundation for Legal Education and its recognition of the value of this publication.

Alan Miller
October 2000

1: A MODERN HUMAN RIGHTS AGENDA

Alan Miller

This opening chapter examines the key provisions of the Scotland Act 1998 and the Human Rights Act 1998, how the Acts interface, and the human rights responsibilities of the Scottish Parliament. The central issue is the requirement to develop a human rights agenda to meet the needs of the 21st century.

WHAT DO THE SCOTLAND ACT AND THE HUMAN RIGHTS ACT REPRESENT?

The two Acts mark the beginning of a modern human rights agenda for Scotland. They provide the elected national body with significant law-making powers and human rights responsibilities as well as constitutional guarantees of a number of significant human rights. They represent an attempt to meet the growing demand in Scotland over the past century for self-determination as a nation and as individual citizens.

'Scottish solutions to Scottish problems' and 'bringing rights home' are the ethos of both Acts. The promise is of 'a new Scotland with new politics', of popular participation, accessibility, openness and consensus. Inevitably, as the Parliament begins to take shape and the European Convention on Human Rights is introduced into our legal and constitutional system, critics are claiming that the reality is not meeting the rhetoric. But setting that aside for a moment, let us examine the implications of both Acts to see how far they may serve the development of a human rights agenda.

THE HUMAN RIGHTS ACT

Both the Scotland Act 1998 and the Human Rights Act 1998 received the Royal Assent in November 1998. For political reasons the commencement of the Scotland Act was accelerated while that of the Human Rights Act was delayed until 2 October 2000. As a result of the earlier commencement of the Scotland Act the effect of sections 29 and 57 of the Scotland Act, requiring the Parliament and the Executive to comply with the European Convention on Human Rights and Fundamental Freedoms (hereafter referred to as 'the ECHR'), has been to create a hiatus which is proving to be problematic. This is best illustrated within our criminal justice system where the limited introduction of the ECHR, following upon the appointment of the Lord Advocate as a member of the Scottish Executive on 20 May 1999 and the consequent compliance requirements placed on the prosecution service, have not been broadly understood and properly integrated. This has masked the potential impact of the ECHR and delayed the change of thinking which will be required, not least by our judiciary, following the commencement of the Human Rights Act.

The effect of the Human Rights Act 1998

The Act is the means whereby the ECHR is given a unique position in our legal and constitutional system. The ECHR has a status higher than an 'ordinary' Act of the Westminster Parliament while falling short of being constitutionally guaranteed within the United Kingdom. So far as the Scottish Parliament and the Scottish Executive are concerned, the ECHR is in effect given a constitutional guarantee in that the Scotland Act 1998 requires the Scottish Parliament and the Scottish Executive to comply with the ECHR as so defined by the Human Rights Act. Strictly speaking, then, the Human Rights Act does not 'incorporate' the ECHR but is 'an Act to give further effect to rights and freedoms guaranteed under the European Convention on Human Rights'.

The significance of this is best understood by way of a brief explanation of the previous status of the ECHR in our legal and constitutional system. In the case of *Kaur v Lord Advocate* 1980 SC 319 Lord Ross stated that a Scottish court was not entitled to take into account the ECHR as it had not been incorporated into our domestic law. This created a rather surreal situation for the next 17 years and is partly responsible for the general lack of preparedness in the legal system for the introduction of the ECHR by the Human Rights Act. It was left to Lord Hope in *T, Petitioner* 1997 SLT 724 to bring Scots law into line with the English position, exemplified by *R v Secretary of State for the Home Department, ex parte Brind* [1991] 1 AC 696, which was essentially that where there was an ambiguity in domestic legislation as to whether it complied or conflicted with the ECHR, the courts should presume that Parliament had intended to legislate in accordance with the ECHR and not in conflict with it. Since then the ECHR has been cited with increasing frequency in Scotland, particularly in the High Court of Justiciary. An example is the case of *McLeod v HM Advocate* 1998 SCCR 77 which sought to decide the question of disclosure in a manner compatible with Art 6 (1) of the ECHR.

Notwithstanding this belated progress the status of the ECHR was nevertheless limited to being no more than an aid to construction. Drafted in 1950 in the aftermath of fascism in Europe, operational since 1953 and with a right of individual petition from the United Kingdom to the European Court of Human Rights in Strasbourg since 1966, the ECHR has only now entered the legal and constitutional systems of the United Kingdom. This was largely due to the lack of a written constitution and to the absolute sovereignty of the Westminster Parliament. Successive United Kingdom governments refused to incorporate the ECHR, considering it to be both unnecessary and an interference with the sovereignty of Westminster. It is against this background that the special status given to the ECHR can be evaluated.

Courts and tribunals in the United Kingdom now 'must take into account', where relevant, the law of the ECHR (s 2(1), Human Rights Act). 'So far as it is possible to do so, primary legislation and subordinate legislation must be read and given effect in a way which is compatible with Convention rights' (s 3(1), Human Rights Act). 'If the court is satisfied that the provision [primary legislation] is incompatible with a Convention right, it may make a declaration of that incompatibility.' (s 4(2), Human Rights Act, with regard to Westminster legislation) and a United Kingdom Minister may, following such a declaration of incompatibility, by order, make such amendments to the primary legislation as he considers necessary (s 10, Human Rights Act—'fast-track remedial procedure'). Additionally, at Westminster a Minister, before the second reading of a Bill, must present a statement regarding the compatibility of the Bill with the ECHR, although it should be noted that the Minister can nevertheless ask Westminster to pass the Bill notwithstanding an admitted incompatibility (s 19, Human Rights Act). It is believed that, in this way, 'honour is satisfied'. It is claimed that 'rights have been brought home' without breaching the absolute sovereignty of the Westminster Parliament.

The giving of 'further effect' to the ECHR is also demonstrated by s 6(1) of the Human Rights Act which declares: 'It is unlawful for a public authority to act in a way which is incompatible with a Convention right.' Section 6(3) states that 'public authority' includes 'a court or tribunal' and a broad range of bodies 'certain of whose functions are functions of a public nature'. The Act does not define 'public authority' and will be for the courts to determine who is and who is not to be so defined. It is likely that the courts will take into account a number of criteria including whether, but for the existence of the body in question, the government would itself intervene to regulate the activity in question; whether the government has provided any underpinning for the activities of the body; and whether the body exercises extensive or monopolistic powers. From this standpoint, therefore, it is anticipated that such bodies as the privatised utilities, Railtrack, Group 4 or the Press Complaints Commission could be defined as 'public authorit[ies]' along with the obvious candidates—for example, local authorities, the police, prisons, immigration authorities and customs and excise.

Section 8 provides for a new range of remedies, relevant to the diversity of anticipated cases, for the 'victim' of a breach of ECHR rights. Section 8(1) declares:

> 'In relation to any act (or proposed act) of a public authority which the court finds is (or would be) unlawful, it may grant such relief or remedy, or make such order, within its powers as it considers just and appropriate.'

Generally speaking, there will be reliance upon ECHR law in such legal proceedings. The proceedings, most likely by means of judicial review, may be initiated by a 'victim' claiming a breach of ECHR rights. The scope of judicial review would no longer be limited to questions of irrationality, illegality or impropriety but expanded to include compatibility with the ECHR and to consider therefore such questions as proportionality. The merits, specific facts and circumstances of certain administrative decisions of public authorities would therefore have to be open to judicial review.

Reliance may also be made on ECHR law in the course of legal proceedings brought by public authorities. A residual right of appeal to the European Court of Human Rights in Strasbourg would remain conditional upon the exhaustion of domestic remedies as before. On 'devolution issues'—that is, *ultra vires* challenges in terms of the Scotland Act—the final appeal lies to the Judicial Committee of the Privy Council.

In short, the Human Rights Act will introduce a significantly greater degree of accountability in public life. Arbitrary exercise of power against the individual will be legally challengeable and the tests of proportionality and legality will be applied. Where two or more public authorities interface or work together they will have to be more accountable to one another. Thus the police and the procurator fiscal service must function so as not to jeopardise effective criminal prosecution. Additionally, the individual will become more accountable to the community in that individual rights under the ECHR, generally speaking, will be weighed against the public interest and a balance struck by the courts.

The Human Rights Act introduces for the first time into our legal system a definitive framework in which the fundamental civil and political rights of the individual are balanced with the public interest. This will develop in all our domestic tribunals and courts and will be widely reported and commented upon by the media. In Canada the Charter of Rights and Freedoms brought about a vibrant voluntary sector, with a broad range of non-governmental organisations supporting 'victims', taking advantage of the new remedies across a host of issues in all branches of law. It is likely that the same will happen here. Quite literally, there is no branch of law which will remain unaffected to some degree or other by the ECHR, as the following examples demonstrate.

— Criminal law—for example, the right to a fair trial relating to all police procedures, including warrants, detention, etc; acts of the procurator fiscal's office, including disclosure, bail, etc; judicial responsibility; victims' rights; prisoners' rights.
— Child and family law—for example, the right to a fair hearing and the right to privacy regarding provision of social services, such as child protection, etc.
— Employment law—for example, the right to a fair hearing; the right to privacy and freedom of association and expression regarding employer/employee relations, such as disciplinary procedures and the new employment tribunal test of 'reasonableness'; whistleblowing; political activity; monitoring of and random drug testing of employees; discrimination; union recognition, etc.
— Privacy law—for example, respect for privacy and family life, home and correspondence; the law relating to media intrusion; CCTV and other forms of surveillance and information gathering; travellers' rights, etc.
— Public law—for example, the rights to a fair hearing and to respect for privacy regarding planning, licensing, welfare benefits, etc.
— Property law—for example, the right to peaceful enjoyment of possession of land regarding compulsory purchase orders; land reform, etc.
— Discrimination—for example, the right not to be subject to discrimination regarding provision of social services such as housing, education, welfare benefits, immigration, sexual orientation, etc.

It is beyond doubt that the Human Rights Act will have a significant effect in creating a culture of rights in an environment which, until now, has provided the state with excessive power and discretion. On the other hand, the continued absence of economic, social and cultural rights and the continued sovereignty of the Westminster Parliament demonstrate that the Human Rights Act alone cannot and should not be expected to meet the requirements of the 21st century.

Thus, from a modern human rights perspective, the Human Rights Act can be seen as an accommodation (perhaps less than comfortable and of a short-term nature) of a mid-20th-century instrument whereby sovereignty resides with Parliament and rights are granted, restricted or denied by that Parliament.

THE INTERFACE BETWEEN THE HUMAN RIGHTS ACT AND THE SCOTLAND ACT

Section 29 (1) of the Scotland Act 1998 states:

> 'An Act of the Scottish Parliament is not law so far as any provision of the Act is outside the legislative competence of the Parliament.'

Section 29 (2) goes on to state:

> 'A provision is outside that competence so far as any of the following paragraphs apply— . . . (d) it is incompatible with any of the Convention Rights or with Community law. . . .'

Section 57 (2) states:

> 'A member of the Scottish Executive has no power to make any subordinate legislation, or to do any other act, so far as the legislation or act is incompatible with any of the Convention rights or with Community law.'

Section 102 (2) states that where the Scottish Parliament or a member of the Scottish Executive has acted outwith their power:

> 'The court or tribunal may make an order—(a) removing or limiting any retrospective effect of the decision, or (b) suspending the effect of the decision for any period, and on any conditions, to allow the defect to be corrected.'

Thus, as far as the Scottish Parliament and Scottish Executive are concerned, the citizens' rights contained in the ECHR are given constitutional guarantees and the Scottish Parliament therefore has a limited sovereignty. This is so because the Scottish Parliament is considered to be a subordinate legislative chamber relative to the Westminster Parliament. The rich irony is that the constitutional tradition of limited sovereignty was in effect subsumed following the Act of Union of 1707 and it is the English constitutional doctrine of the absolute sovereignty of Parliament which has prevailed within the United Kingdom ever since.

A consequence of the Scotland Act is that human rights, presently in the somewhat limited shape of the ECHR, will enjoy a more enhanced status in Scotland than in the rest of the United Kingdom.

It is to be expected that the question will be raised as to why no similar status has been given to the economic, social and cultural rights provided by the United Nations international human rights treaties already ratified by the United Kingdom. In a sense it is a question which is already tabled. In 1993 the United Nations World Conference on Human Rights in Vienna issued a declaration affirming the universality, indivisibility and interdependence of civil, political, economic, social and cultural rights. More specifically in 1997 the UN Committee on Economic, Social and Cultural Rights[1] included among its concluding observations to the United Kingdom the following:

---

[1] Concluding observations of the UN Committee on Economic, Social and Cultural Rights regarding the Third Periodic Report published in Geneva, 7 December 1997. See also the Human Rights Responsibilities of the Scottish Parliament and United Nations, 17 November 1997, presented to the above Committee by Professor Alan Miller, Director of the Scottish Human Rights Centre, and published by the Centre.

'The Committee finds disturbing the position of the State [the UK] party that provisions of the Covenant [the International Covenant on Economic, Social and Cultural Rights of 1966], with certain minor exceptions, constitute principles and pragmatic objectives rather than legal obligations, and that consequently the provisions of the Covenant cannot be given legislative effect.'

The Committee proceeded to recommend that:

'the State party take appropriate steps to introduce into legislation the Covenant on Economic, Social and Cultural Rights, so that the rights covered by the Covenant may be fully implemented. It is encouraged that the State party has taken such action with respect to the European Convention on Human Rights and is of the view that it would be appropriate to give similar due regard to the obligations of the Covenant.'

Although the ratification of international human rights treaties is reserved to the United Kingdom Parliament in terms of the Scotland Act, Sched 5, para 7(1), it is significant that para 7(2) states that not reserved are '(a) observing and implementing international obligations, obligations under the Human Rights Convention and obligations under Community law . . .'. It is clear, therefore, that the Scottish Parliament has definite responsibilities to observe and implement the provisions of such ratified international human rights treaties as the International Covenant on Economic, Social and Cultural Rights 1966, the International Covenant on Civil and Political Rights 1966, the UN Convention on the Elimination of All Forms of Discrimination Against Women 1979 and the UN Convention on the Rights of the Child 1989, etc.

With regard to human rights compatibility, any Bill introduced in the Scottish Parliament should include a considered assessment as to the implementation of the rights contained in the ratified United Nations human rights treaties. Of note is a further recommendation of the UN Committee on Economic, Social and Cultural Rights 1997[2] that:

'consideration be given to the requirement that a Human Rights Assessment or Impact Statement be made an integral part of every proposed legislation or policy initiative on a basis analogous to Environmental Impact Assessment or Statements'.

In this regard ss 35 and 58 of the Scotland Act may have some relevance. Section 35 provides that the Secretary of State may intervene to make an order prohibiting the presentation of a Bill of the Scottish Parliament for Royal Assent in circumstances where the Bill may be incompatible with international obligations. Similarly, s 58 gives the Secretary of State power to intervene to prevent or require action (including the introduction of a Bill in the Scottish Parliament) by a member of the Scottish Executive to ensure compatibility with international obligations.

---

[2] See note 1.

As far as the development of a modern human rights agenda is concerned, the form by which the Scotland Act and the Human Rights Act combine to give further effect in Scotland to the ECHR may ultimately be of much more significance than the impact of the content of the ECHR.

The interface between the Scotland Act and the Human Rights Act may also have consequences for the governance of the United Kingdom and future relations between the Scottish Parliament and the Westminster Parliament. Unlike the Scotland Bill of 1978 the Scotland Act gives a general power of competence to the Scottish Parliament with Sched 5 providing a list, albeit lengthy, of powers reserved to Westminster.

The effect of Sched 5 on some of the specified powers reserved to Westminster and the continued sovereignty of Westminster *vis-à-vis* the ECHR pose some questions only time may answer. For example, Sched 5, section L2, reserves:

> 'Equal opportunities, including the subject-matter of—(a) the Equal Pay Act 1970, (b) the Sex Discrimination Act 1975, (c) the Race Relations Act 1976, and (d) the Disability Discrimination Act 1995.'

This is already seen as an anomaly, given the breadth of devolved areas where equal opportunities legislation has an impact and given the requirement for the Scottish Parliament and the Scottish Executive to act in a manner compatible with the ECHR which, of course, itself includes a provision against discrimination in art 14.

Equally, the protection of human rights, particularly in terms of art 3 (prohibition against torture, inhumane and degrading treatment), art 6 (the right to a fair and public hearing) and art 8 (the right to respect for private and family life, home and correspondence) has considerable implications for a whole range of matters reserved under Sched 5 such as social security, employment and immigration, etc. What if, in the Court of Session, Westminster Parliament legislation is found to breach the ECHR in such reserved areas and the fast-track remedial procedure at Westminster is not exercised, thus weakening human rights protection in Scotland? One can imagine the dilemma for the Scots lawyer advising the mystified client: 'Well, on the one hand, you may well win in Edinburgh because the court may recognise your right under the ECHR. But, on the other hand, you may actually lose the case because, at the end of the day, it is up to Westminster and it is Westminster law which must prevail over the ECHR until, once you have won your case in Strasbourg, Westminster changes the law.'

The definition of reserved powers is not fixed in stone and s 63 of the Scotland Act provides a mechanism for the transfer of functions from United Kingdom Ministers to Scottish Ministers by Order in Council. There is also nothing in the Scotland Act to prevent the Scottish Parliament debating any matter, be it devolved or reserved. What, then, if the Scottish Parliament debates certain economic and social rights, perhaps in the context of a review of the social security system or disability benefit entitlements, and wishes certain legislation to be passed by Westminster in such reserved areas? What if Westminster either chooses not to legislate or passes its legislation contrary to the will of the Scottish Parliament? What if the Scottish Parliament considers that this is a breach of the ECHR or another international human rights treaty and seeks to have a transfer of function to the Scottish Executive and Westminster is not prepared to effect the transfer?

Section 103 of the Scotland Act provides that the Judicial Committee of the Privy Council will be the arbiter of disputes regarding 'devolution issues' concerning the powers of the Scottish Parliament. Inevitably some of such issues will be politically and constitutionally sensitive. Just as inevitably, the appropriateness of such a body determining such sensitive matters will be called into question, not least the manner of appointment and accountability of its members. The inevitability of such questioning is underlined by the fact that the appointment of the Scottish judiciary is already under scrutiny since the Scotland Act provides further powers to the Scottish judges and gives the Scottish Parliament a role in their removal, but no role as yet in their appointment. The sustainability of the Judicial Committee of the Privy Council as arbiter of devolution issues is an open question and the establishment of a modern constitutional court arbitrating disputes between Stormont, Cardiff, Edinburgh and Westminster seems only a matter of time.

In summary, an effect of the Scotland Act and the Human Rights Act may be to create not a modern national Bill of Rights for Scotland but a 'notional' Bill of Rights, composed of the ECHR, with the Scottish Parliament supplying additional rights and implementing, within its competence, the rights contained in the UN human rights treaties ratified by the United Kingdom. It is, therefore, very much an open question whether the Scottish Parliament will have the competence to enable it to adopt a modern national Bill of Rights encompassing the areas which are currently reserved to Westminster.

THE SCOTLAND ACT AND THE HUMAN RIGHTS ACT: THE EMERGENCE OF A MODERN DEMOCRATIC SCOTTISH PERSONALITY?

The answers to the questions posed above relating to the governance of the United Kingdom and relations in the field of human rights between Edinburgh and London depend in part upon what sort of modern democratic Scottish personality emerges and the extent to which it seeks to assert itself. It may be that arrangements have yet to evolve whereby the diverse traditions and aspirations within the different jurisdictions in these islands find a natural and modern expression. In order to understand and be prepared to address such potential developments it is instructive to look at some of the factors which will help to shape the modern democratic Scottish personality. Some of these factors—such as the distinctive traditions and aspirations—are internal, and some—for example, the European and international framework within which a devolved Scotland is emerging—are external.

For both contemporary and historical reasons the Scottish Parliament is likely to adopt a more favourable approach to human rights than has been taken by the Westminster Parliament, and this will inevitably have implications for the governance of Scotland and the United Kingdom.

The political composition and working procedures of the Scottish Parliament are different from those of Westminster in a number of respects. First, there is a form of proportional representation in the electoral system and its proponents claim that the fact that no one party is likely to have an overall majority will result in time in a less adversarial, more consensual and reasoned legislative approach. Secondly, there is a powerful committee system in which all-party committees, reflecting the political balance within the Parliament, have powers not only to scrutinise the Executive but also to initiate legislation following full and effective consultation with expert bodies and the public at large. Thirdly, there is predominantly a four-party system, with the addition of a significant number of independents, and all the parties deem it electorally necessary to assert their 'Scottish identity'. The distinctive Scottish identity and tradition on rights— expressed today as rights belonging inalienably to each of us by dint of our humanity—and on sovereignty— expressed today as sovereignty lying with the people and not Parliament— are bound to influence the personality of the Scottish Parliament and its approach to human rights.

In analysing the potential impact of the Scotland Act and the Human Rights Act on the governance of Scotland and of the United Kingdom a critical issue is the extent to which the Scottish perspectives on rights and sovereignty are reflected in the Scottish personality emerging as a result of devolution. Let us therefore look briefly at those perspectives.

The Scottish perspective on rights

Contrary to certain proposals human rights were, quite rationally, not listed as a reserved matter as such. The Scotland Act is broadly based on the Scottish Constitutional Convention's blueprint,[3] *Scotland's Parliament, Scotland's Right*, which among other things proposed a Charter of Rights for Scotland

> 'advancing clear principles and specifying their rights and freedoms held to be inviolable . . . to encompass and improve upon prevailing international law and the Conventions [the ECHR, ICCPR, European Parliament's Declaration of Fundamental Rights and Freedoms, etc] and to be firmly based on Scottish traditions and values'.

The 1997 General Election Manifesto of the Scottish Labour Party stated that the Scottish Parliament

> 'will also be empowered to give special additional protection to fundamental rights and freedoms in Scots law . . . citizens should have statutory rights to enforce their human rights in the UK courts . . . the incorporation of the ECHR will establish a floor, not a ceiling, for human rights'.

Such documents reflect, and indeed in some respect borrow, the language of the 1992 draft Bill of Rights for Scotland[4] following a broad consultation process involving the major political and civic bodies in Scotland. These documents do no

---

[3] The Constitutional Convention held its inaugural meeting on 30 March 1989 and adopted a Claim of Right which was signed by all members. This Claim of Right was the third in Scotland's history, and its purpose was 'to root the Convention solidly in an historic Scottish Constitutional principle that power is limited, should be dispersed and is derived from the people'.
[4] A Bill of Rights for Scotland was published by the Scottish Council for Civil Liberties (since renamed the Scottish Human Rights Centre).

more than give expression to an historic and distinctively Scottish perspective on rights. The essence of this perspective, unlike the English or Anglo-American notion, is that an individual's right is seen as a 'right to personality'. The individual's personality, rights and duties are understood as being dependent not upon the grant of the state but upon the enjoyment of such rights by the community as a whole with which the individual interacts. Accordingly, the degree of freedom or emancipation of an individual is dependent not upon the grant of the state but upon the extent of freedom or emancipation of the people, of society, as a whole. It is this understanding—of the individual not standing alone but as a member of a society—which recognises the inalienable right to that agreed level of social and economic provision required by the individual to exercise political and civil rights and fully participate in society.

This Scottish tradition is consistent with the contemporary international understanding, reaffirmed at the World Human Rights Conference in Vienna in 1993, that civil, political and economic and social rights are universal, indivisible, interrelated and interdependent. It also accords with what people actually understand as their rights today: the right of livelihood, the right to the highest possible provision of public services, the right of effective participation in public affairs, etc. This was reflected in the vote in the Scottish constitutional referendum on 11 September 1998, when the overwhelming majority voted in favour not only of a Scottish Parliament, but also for tax-varying powers to address economic and social needs.

A modern expression of this tradition is that such rights belong to all of us by dint of our very humanity and this is why they may be termed human rights. If society is to progress, enabling its resources to meet today's demands, such a definition is required. It flows from this that the purpose of a country enshrining human rights in its constitution, or of ratifying an international human rights treaty, is that its parliament is mandated to pass effective legislation not only in the civil and political fields but also in the economic and social fields.

The recommendation of the UN Committee on Economic, Social and Cultural Rights referred to earlier, that legislative effect be given not only to the ECHR but also to the International Covenant on Economic, Social and Cultural Rights, may well be supported by a Scottish Parliament but may prove difficult for a Westminster Parliament rooted in the 18th-century definition of rights and sovereignty.

The Scottish perspective on sovereignty

The Scottish perspective on sovereignty naturally complements the approach to rights described above and was notably expressed by Lord President Cooper in the case of *MacCormick* v *Lord Advocate* 1953 SC 396:

> 'The principle of unlimited sovereignty of Parliament is a distinctively English principle which has no counterpart in Scottish constitutional law. It derives its origin from Coke and Blackstone and was widely popularised during the 19th century by Bagehot and Dicey, the latter having stated the doctrine in its classic form in his Law of the Constitutions. Considering that the Union legislation extinguished the Parliaments of Scotland and England

and replaced them by a new Parliament, I had difficulty in seeing why it should be supposed that the new Parliament of Great Britain must inherit all the peculiar characteristics of the English Parliament but none of the Scottish Parliament, as if all that happened in 1707 was that Scottish representatives were admitted to the Parliament of England. That is not what was done.'

The historic approach in Scotland of 'power within limits' finds a modern expression in the Claim of Right of the Scottish Constitutional Convention which declares:

'We gathered as the Scottish Constitutional Convention, do hereby acknowledge the sovereign right of the Scottish people to determine the form of government best suited to their needs, and do hereby declare and pledge that in all our actions and deliberations their interests shall be paramount.'

As with the question of rights, this perspective is consistent with the contemporary universal experience that sovereignty lies with the people and that this is a condition of the progress of any modern society. The Scotland Act fails to reflect this, acknowledging that sovereignty remains at Westminster. Having said that, introducing the Bill to the Westminster Parliament, the then Secretary of State for Scotland, Donald Dewar, MP, confirmed what is broadly recognised across the Scottish political spectrum that, in the final analysis, the political reality is that sovereignty does reside, in fact, with the people of Scotland.

THE SCOTLAND ACT AND THE HUMAN RIGHTS ACT: AN INTERNATIONAL ROLE FOR SCOTLAND?

If this distinctive tradition on rights and sovereignty is a determining influence on a modern Scottish personality, there is no escaping the fact that the personality that emerges will be significantly affected by external factors.

The rapidly developing European and international dimension has an impact on every aspect of modern life and society, no more so than in the field of rights and sovereignty. This is evidenced by the ever-increasing influence of the European Union itself, the ECHR, the European Social Charter and the range of international human rights treaties, conventions and institutions. It is into this real world that Scotland is now proceeding and it is only within this context that the significance of the Human Rights Act and the Scotland Act and their impact on the governance of Scotland and the United Kingdom can be understood.

There are already a number of illustrations of the recognition of a significant potential international role for Scotland. Not least among them was the Inaugural Scottish Symposium on Human Rights held on 11 June 1999 which produced a report entitled 'Rights here, rights now, the place of human rights in the government of a modern Scotland'.[5] The United Nations Special Advisor on National Institutions to the High Commissioner for Human Rights, Brian Burdekin, outlined to the Symposium, including the Deputy First Minister and

---

[5] 'Report on the Inaugural Scottish Symposium on Human Rights', published by the Scottish Human Rights Centre.

Justice Minister, Jim Wallace, and other MSPs, the important role that at this particular juncture of its historical development Scotland, and specifically a Scottish Human Rights Commission, could play in providing an international model for the advancement of civil, political, economic, social and cultural rights.

As we survey the international scene at the dawn of a new millennium, one thing above all is striking—the requirement in the 21st century of a modern definition of human rights. As in the 18th century, an impasse has been reached and humanity's progress is being held back. Quite literally a defining moment has been reached, and it is here that Scotland's greatest contribution may lie.

If in the 18th century it was the claim against the old feudal order of the ascending class of industrialists and merchants to gain access to society's existing and potential resources, today it is the claim of society to progress by humanising the natural and social environment. Rousseau and other thinkers of the Enlightenment provided a definition of rights and sovereignty—'liberty, equality and fraternity'—which enabled the new economic and social forces to come to power and affirm their property rights. Since these great achievements two centuries have passed, filled with the turmoil of growth and development, reflected in all spheres of society. The end of the 20th century has witnessed the arrival of property rights and human rights competing as to which should be placed at the centre of development of society.

To understand the present it is helpful to pay regard to international developments in the second half of the 20th century. Following the victory over fascism in World War Two and in recognition of the need for the international protection of human rights, a statement of rights was adopted by the United Nations in 1948 in the form of the Universal Declaration of Human Rights. This was to be 'a common standard of achievement for all peoples and nations'.[6] In 1966 the United Nations adopted two general statements of human rights in the form of treaties binding on the ratifying states, namely the International Covenant on Civil and Political Rights and the International Covenant on Economic, Social and Cultural Rights. Since then the United Nations has created a variety of human rights conventions, particularly in the field of collective rights and anti-discrimination. Significant conventions include the International Convention on Elimination of All Forms of Racial Discrimination 1966, the International Convention on the Elimination of All Forms of Discrimination Against Women 1979 and the United Nations Convention on the Rights of the Child 1989.

Commentators often divide internationally protected human rights into three 'generations', reflecting their historical development and also the divisions between the economic and political powers which, until this last decade, dominated the world stage.

The so-called 'first generation' of human rights are those with which we in Western Europe are most familiar in that some of them are to be found in the European Convention on Human Rights as well as in the International Covenant on Civil and Political Rights. Typically, they include the right to life, the right to personal liberty, the right not to be subjected to slavery, torture or inhumane or degrading treatment or punishment, and a range of 'due process' rights, including the right to a fair trial. This generation also includes the right to privacy and respect for family life, freedom of expression, thought, conscience and religion,

---

[6] Eleanor Roosevelt, Chair of the United Nations Human Rights Commission.

the right to peaceful assembly and association, and the right to participate in the governance of one's own country.

The 'second generation' recognises economic, social and cultural rights. It includes rights to an adequate standard of living, to food, clothing and housing, the right to be free from hunger,[7] the right to the highest attainable standard of physical and mental health, the right to education (at least to primary standard), the right to take part in the cultural life of the community, and the right to enjoy the benefits of scientific progress and its applications.[8]

The 'third generation' includes rights to self-determination, to development, to equality of all peoples to dispose of their wealth and natural resources freely, to international peace and security,[9] and to a satisfactory environment.

At the time of the Cold War a hierarchy of rights came into being. Human rights became an ideological prisoner of this conflict and a pretext for advancing competing geopolitical ambitions. After the Cold War human rights began to be seen in an integrated way, as the means of solving problems facing humanity, and no longer as mere aspirations or ideological weapons.

Throughout the last decade, World Conferences, such as those in Rio, known as the Earth Summit, in Rome on Food and in Beijing on Women, have served to place on the agenda the need for a modern definition of human rights to be advanced if the problems facing humanity are to be addressed. However, the Earth Summit could not remove from the developing countries the crippling burden of debt, the Food Conference could not give food to the masses of humanity and the Women's Conference could only recognise the degraded status of women. It was not the lack of resources, voting rights or human rights which counted but the property rights of those wielding economic and political power. At Rome the US representative proclaimed contempt for international human rights treaties by declaring that 'there is no right to food'. It is now widely recognised in the United Nations and among the increasingly influential numbers of non-governmental organisations that, notwithstanding the progress which has been made in the 50 years since the Universal Declaration of Human Rights in 1948, the United Nations Covenants and enforcement mechanisms are too far removed from people's lives and have proven to be weak in the face of economic and political power. They have been unable, generally speaking, to provide the necessities of life to masses of humanity, let alone tackle the marginalisation of people from the decision-making process in their own countries and internationally. This has become all the more evident with the development of the global economy which has weakened the nation states—the supposed protectors of the human rights of their citizens in terms of the treaties ratified by them.

---

[7] The United Nations Universal Declaration on the Eradication of Hunger and Malnutrition, adopted on 16 November 1974 by the World Food Conference convened under General Assembly resolution 3180 (XXVIII) of 17 December 1973 and endorsed by General Assembly resolution 3348 (XXIX) of 17 December 1974.

[8] See, for example, the United Nations Declaration on the Use of Scientific and Technological Progress in the Interests of Peace and for the Benefit of Mankind, proclaimed by General Assembly resolution 3384 (XXXX) of 10 November 1975 and the United Nations Declaration of the Principles of International Culture Co-operation, proclaimed by the General Conference of the United Nations Education, Scientific and Cultural Organisation at its 14th session on 4 November 1966.

[9] See, for example, the United Nations Declaration on the Right of Peoples to Peace, approved by General Assembly resolution 39/11 of 12 November 1984.

The need for change was reflected in part at the 1993 Vienna United Nations World Conference on Human Rights, which declared:

> 'All human rights (civil, political, economic, social and cultural) are universal, indivisible and inter-dependent and inter-related. The international community must treat human rights globally in a fair and equal manner, on the same footing, and with the same emphasis.'

Later in 1993, following the Vienna Declaration and programme of action, the General Assembly of the United Nations established the post of the United Nations High Commissioner on Human Rights (currently filled by the former President of the Irish Republic, Mary Robinson) and proclaimed a Human Rights Education Decade to begin in 1994, with a review of progress to be made in 1998, the 50th anniversary of the Universal Declaration of Human Rights.

What is required is a recognition and understanding that we all possess rights (civil, political, economic, social and cultural) by dint of our very humanity and that they are inalienable. Thus what it means to be a human being is integral to the development of society and is not merely an aspiration or long-term objective.

This can be seen as a modern expression of Scotland's distinctive tradition and philosophy on rights and sovereignty as previously outlined. The Scotland Act and the Human Rights Act are an attempt to meet the demand for self-determination—as a nation and as citizens—and what now develops in Scotland at this defining moment has a potentially significant impact internationally.

Global developments and Scotland's own experience have vividly demonstrated that the critical questions are: how is effect to be given to a modern definition of human rights, how is it to be affirmed?

Rights cannot be affirmed without the ability to exercise power to give effect to them. It is a modern human right, one leading to the solution of today's problems, to participate in the governance of one's country and in the decision-making process.

Since the end of the Cold War a period of democratic renewal has been ushered in. It necessarily begins in the internal political processes and encompasses the relations between nations and international institutions—not least the United Nations itself. Accordingly, renewal of democracy involves vesting sovereignty or political power in the citizenry, defining their rights and duties and those they give to their elected representatives and governments.

There is no grand formula and each people will find its own way consistent with its own traditions and conditions. Scotland, however, is ideally suited to become a standard-bearer. A small nation with a legacy from the Age of Enlightenment out of all proportion to its size, it has an identity as one of the most ancient nations and has no problems of unrest or ethnicity. Standing within the Westminster parliamentary system it has a European and Commonwealth identity and is now assuming the responsibilities of implementing the United Nations international human rights treaties.

The unfolding of this self-determination, this renewed assertion of identity as a people and as individual citizens is potentially of profound international significance. The emergence of a modern Scottish personality, developing a modern human rights agenda, may shed a light far beyond its borders.

CONCLUSION

What is the verdict on the Scotland Act and the Human Rights Act? Who is right—the critics who claim the reality has not matched the rhetoric or the promoters who claim they have already met the demand for self-determination? Both claims may prove to be premature. The practical point at this stage is that the Acts could open the door towards the development of a modern human rights agenda. The history of the 21st century will record the true significance of the Scotland Act and the Human Rights Act.

2: INTERNATIONAL HUMAN RIGHTS IN A DEVOLVED SCOTLAND

Rebecca M M Wallace and Kenneth Dale-Risk

INTRODUCTION

The raison d'être of this chapter is to examine the Scottish Parliament's responsibility for implementing international obligations with respect to human rights. The chapter will spell out the legislative competence of the Scottish Parliament in this area and will identify any restriction imposed on this competence. In particular the legislative competence to give effect internally to international human rights obligations assumed by the UK Executive by way of treaty[1] will be examined. Consideration will be given to any potential problems which may ensue and, in conclusion, the chapter will focus on the mechanisms which may be employed to develop a human rights culture in Scotland.

THE SCOTTISH PARLIAMENT'S LEGISLATIVE COMPETENCE AS PRESCRIBED IN THE SCOTLAND ACT 1998

The Scottish Parliament has legislative competence in matters which are not reserved to Westminster. Reserved matters in the field of foreign affairs are identified in Schedule 5, paragraph 7(1) of the Scotland Act[2] as extending to 'International relations, including relations with territories outside the United Kingdom, the European Communities (and their institutions) and other international organisations, regulation of international trade, and international development assistance and co-operation.'

This is qualified so as not to reserve 'observance and implementation of international obligations, obligations under the Human Rights Convention and obligations under Community law[3] or assisting Ministers of the Crown in relation to any matter to which Paragraph 7(1) applies.'

As is apparent, the Scottish Parliament has legislative competence in the observance of international obligations. This is not, however, an unfettered competence and is subject to a number of restrictions. These restrictions are contained in section 29, section 35 and section 57.

In accordance with section 29(1) and (2)(d) an Act of the Scottish Parliament will

---

[1] Although a treaty is the principal vehicle employed for the protection of human rights in contemporary international society international rights obligations may arise from customary international law. In many instances customary international law will reflect an obligation originally enshrined in a treaty, eg genocide.
[2] 1998, cap 46.
[3] Para 7(2)(a).

not be law to the extent that it is incompatible with any Convention right.[4] The role of the Scottish judiciary in relation to section 29(1) will be examined further, not least because the section highlights a difference in approach from that which will be taken to legislation emanating from Westminster.

In terms of section 35(1), if a Bill of the Scottish Parliament appears, in the view of the Secretary of State,[5] to be incompatible with any international obligations, the Secretary of State may make an order prohibiting the submission of the Bill for the Royal Assent.[6] The practical effect is that the Secretary of State at Westminster will enjoy the power of veto over primary legislation of the Scottish Parliament.

In relation to secondary legislation, in terms of section 58, if the Secretary of State has reasonable grounds to believe that any action proposed to be taken by a member of the Scottish Executive would be incompatible with any international obligations, he may direct that the proposed actions shall not be taken.[7] Alternatively if the Secretary of State has reasonable grounds to believe that any action capable of being taken by a member of the Scottish Executive is required for the purpose of giving effect to such obligations,[8] he may by order direct that the action shall be taken.[9] If any subordinate legislation made or which could be revoked by a member of the Scottish Executive contains provisions which the Secretary of State has reasonable grounds to believe would be incompatible with any international obligations, he may by order revoke the legislation.[10]

Thus the Scottish Parliament has a responsibility to honour international obligations but it is a responsibility which is to be exercised under the supervision of Westminster. In practice the effect of the controls imposed will be that in promulgating legislation the Scottish Parliament must give cognisance to fulfilling the international obligations incumbent on the United Kingdom. Nor can the Scottish Parliament exonerate itself from compliance with international obligations on the grounds that foreign affairs are a matter reserved to Westminster. In the event of such cognisance not being given the Secretary of State is competent under sections 35 and 58 to intervene.

It appears that the inclusion of sections 35 and 58 is an attempt to avoid the problems which may arise where a division of legislative competence creates the appearance of a quasi-federal state in place of a unitary state. The essence of the problem is that an external competence may not be reflected in an internal competence. In other words a state may undertake international obligations in subject-matter outwith its internal competence and thereby is unable to give internal effect to the obligations assumed.

However, on the international stage such an argument will not exonerate a state from non-compliance with international obligations. A state may not successfully plead either the presence or the absence of domestic law as a defence for non-adherence to international obligations. '[a] State which has contracted valid

---

[4] 'Convention right' has the same meaning as in the Human Rights Act 1998: Scotland Act 1998, s 112(1).
[5] The 'Secretary of State' is *any* secretary of state.
[6] Scotland Act 1998, s 35(1).
[7] s 58(1).
[8] International obligations means any obligations of the United Kingdom other than obligations (a) under Community law, or (b) not to do acts incompatible with any of the Convention rights.
[9] s 58(2).
[10] s 58(4)(a).

international obligations is bound to make in its legislation such modifications as may be necessary to ensure the fulfilment of the obligations undertaken.'[11]

> 'In a unitary State whose legislature possesses unlimited powers the problem is simple. Parliament will fulfil or not treaty obligations imposed upon the State by its executive. The nature of the obligations does not affect the complete authority of the Legislature to make them law if it so chooses . . . in a federal State where legislative authority is limited . . ., or is divided up between different Legislatures, the problem is complex. . . . The question is not how is the obligation formed, that is the function of the executive; but how is the obligation to be performed'.[12]

In that case, *Attorney-General for Canada* v *Attorney-General for Ontario*, legislation designed to give internal effect to draft conventions adopted by the International Labour Organisation and the League of Nations was alleged to be invalid as the Dominion Parliament did not possess the competency to legislate on the subject-matter concerned.

It was the limited internal competence of the Federal Government which delayed the accession of Canada to the UN Covenant on Economic, Social and Cultural Rights and the Covenant on Civil and Political Rights until 1976.

The problems associated with a division in competencies are not familiar in the United Kingdom. One illustration of the possibility of conflict between external and internal competencies is found in *Tyrer* v *United Kingdom*.[13] The case was initiated by the applicant after he was sentenced to three strokes of the birch by a juvenile court in the Isle of Man. The relevant issue in this context is the position of the United Kingdom, its responsibility for the international relations of the Isle of Man.[14] The United Kingdom was required by the European Court of Human Rights to answer the case initiated before the Court on the use of the birch in the Isle of Man. This was the situation even though the United Kingdom had abolished the use on mainland Britain of judicial corporal punishment in the Criminal Justice Act 1948. The European Court of Human Rights in *Tyrer* found against the United Kingdom[15] and unanimously denied the existence of any local

---

[11] *Exchange of Greek and Turkish Populations Case* PCIJ Rep, Ser B, No 10, p 20 (1925). See also *Alabama Claims Arbitration* Moor, 1 Int Arb 495 (1872) and Article 13 of the Draft Declaration on the Rights and Duties of States 1949 whereby 'Each State has the duty to carry out in good faith its obligations, arising from treaties and other sources of international law, and it may not invoke provisions in its constitution or its laws as an excuse for failure to perform this duty.'
[12] *Attorney-General for Canada* v *Attorney-General for Ontario* [1937] AC 326 at p 352.
[13] [1978] 2 EHRR 1.
[14] The Isle of Man legislature, the Court of Tynwald, legislated in domestic matters subject to ratification by the Queen in Council, the Home Secretary being responsible for advising the Privy Council. However, by constitutional convention, the UK Parliament did not exercise its competence to legislate on the island's domestic affairs without the island's consent. This convention could be overridden by an international treaty obligation, however the United Kingdom since 1950 did not regard international treaties applicable to the United Kingdom as extending to the Isle of Man unless there was an express inclusion. In 1953 a letter was sent to the Secretary-General of the Council of Europe by the United Kingdom to the effect that ECHR should extend to the Isle of Man in accordance with Article 63.1.
[15] The Court held by six votes to one that the judicial corporal punishment inflicted on the applicant amounted to degrading punishment within the meaning of Article 3 of the Convention.

requirements[16] within the Isle of Man which could affect the application of Article 3 of the European Convention on Human Rights and Fundamental Freedoms.

THE LEGISLATIVE COMPETENCE OF THE SCOTTISH PARLIAMENT *VIS-À-VIS* INTERNATIONAL HUMAN RIGHTS OBLIGATIONS

How does the legislative competence of the Scottish Parliament square with meeting international human rights obligations? To answer this question it is necessary to examine the principal international human rights obligations incumbent on the United Kingdom.

International obligations are assumed by the executive by way of the royal prerogative and treaty obligations only become part of UK domestic law if incorporated by way of a legislative provision designed specifically for that purpose. For example, the Genocide Act 1969 made the offence characterised as 'genocide' in Article II of the United Nations Convention on the Prevention and Punishment of the Crime of Genocide 1948 an offence in English law, whereas the 1951 Geneva Convention Relating to the Status of Refugees has not been incorporated into UK domestic law.[17] Notwithstanding this, international standards may be utilised as a yardstick and may be reflected in provisions of domestic legislation, eg the Race Relations Act 1976 making discrimination on the ground of race unlawful.

European Convention on Human Rights and Fundamental Freedoms[18]

The distinctive feature of the European Convention on Human Rights and Fundamental Freedoms is that it has at the heart of its enforcement mechanism a judicial organ, the European Court of Human Rights,[19] and that body has been responsible for a substantial volume of jurisprudence on the Convention. However, a further distinction is that the Human Rights Act which received the Royal Assent on 9 November 1998 will incorporate the Convention into UK law. The effect of this will be that individuals who allege that their rights under the Convention have been violated may seek to enforce these rights in the British courts rather than initiating proceedings in Europe after having exhausted all domestic remedies.

What will be the effect of the incorporation of the European Convention in post-devolution Scotland? As has been mentioned earlier an Act of the Scottish Parliament is not law insofar as it is outside its legislative competence. Such would be the case if an Act were incompatible with any of the Convention rights. A proponent of a Bill introduced to the Scottish Parliament must state that it is within the legislative competence of the Parliament and that, by inference, entails that the Bill is compatible with Convention rights. Notwithstanding this, the Court of Session or the High Court of Justiciary could hold the Act to be

---

[16] Article 63(3) provides that the Convention is to be applied within territories for whose international obligations a state is responsible but that this should be with due regard to local requirements.
[17] Nevertheless UK asylum legislation does require that cognisance be given to the Convention.
[18] 213 UNTS 221; TS 71 (1953); Cmd 8969.
[19] Which now sits as a permanent body since the coming into effect of Protocol 11, November 1998.

unlawful[20] on the basis that it is incompatible with Convention rights and accordingly outwith Parliament's legislative competence.

In contrast, if a provision of a Westminster Act were found to be incompatible with the Convention, the Court of Session or the High Court of Justiciary could only make a declarator of incompatibility.[21] Such a declarator will not affect the continuing operation of the provision but it is envisaged that it would precipitate an amendment of the offending legislation.[22] Thus an Act promulgated in Edinburgh can be struck down whereas an Act of the Westminster Parliament is subject only to a declaration of incompatibility. At the root of this distinction lies the desire to protect the sovereignty of the Westminster Parliament.

The cumulative effect of the Scotland Act and the Human Rights Act is to impose on the Scottish judiciary a responsibility to decide on the lawfulness of legislation. This responsibility may be more easily borne by the current incumbents, who have come a long way since the case of *Kaur v Lord Advocate*:

> 'If the Convention does not form part of the municipal law, I do not see why the Court should have regard to it at all. It was His Majesty's Government in 1950 which was a High Contracting Party to the Convention. The Convention has been ratified by the United Kingdom but . . . its provisions cannot be regarded as having the force of law .... Under our Constitution it is the Queen in Parliament who legislates and not Her Majesty's Government, and the Court does not require to have regard to acts of Her Majesty's Government when interpreting the law.'[23]

The European Convention on Human Rights and Fundamental Freedoms is to play a significant role within domestic judicial proceedings. In terms of the Human Rights Act 1998:

> 'A court or tribunal determining a question which has arisen in connection with a Convention right must take into account any—
>
> (a) judgment, decision, declaration or advisory opinion of the European Court of Human Rights,
> (b) opinion of the Commission given in a report adopted under Article 31 of the Convention,
> (c) decision of the Commission in connection with Article 26 or 27(2) of the Convention, or
> (d) decision of the Committee of Ministers taken under Article 46 of the Convention ...'.[24]

This demands more than just a cursory knowledge of the Convention and the

---

[20] Scotland Act, s 29.
[21] Human Rights Act 1998, s 4.
[22] Human Rights Act 1998, s 10.
[23] *Kaur v Lord Advocate* 1981 SLT 322 at p 329 (Lord Ross). See *obiter dicta* of Lord Hope in *T, Petitioner* 1996 SCLR 897 at pp 910–911. This does not deny the existence of a 'prima facie presumption that Parliament does not intend to act in breach of international law, including therein specific treaty obligations': *Salomon v Commissioners of Customs and Excise* [1967] 2 QB 116 at p 143, Lord Diplock, CA.
[24] s 2(1).

Other international human rights instruments

There is a risk that, given the high profile which the European Convention has received in the wake of the Human Rights Act, other international instruments and obligations will not receive the cognisance warranted or indeed demanded by the Scotland Act.[25] There are human rights other than those spelt out in the European Convention. The rights and freedoms protected under the European Convention are only one species of human rights and those other international human rights are arguably, and certainly in the overall global context, as important. It would be in the interest of the individual to have comparable scrutiny of proposed and existing legislation in the light of those other human rights and similar recourse to domestic courts.

The United Kingdom's human rights obligations flow from an increasing number of international instruments. International human rights instruments have proliferated during the fifty years since the signing of the Universal Declaration of Human Rights in 1948.[26] The United Kingdom is a party to a wide range of international human rights instruments of which the following are only a sample: the United Nations Covenant on Civil and Political Rights 1966,[27] the International Covenant on Economic, Social and Cultural Rights 1966,[28] the International Convention on the Elimination of All Forms of Racial Discrimination 1966,[29] Convention on the Elimination of All Forms of Discrimination Against Women 1979,[30] Convention Against Torture and Other Cruel, Inhuman or Degrading Treatment or Punishment 1984,[31] Convention on the Rights of the Child 1989.[32]

The International Covenant on Economic, Social and Cultural Rights enunciates that 'all peoples have the right of self-determination',[33] and recognises 'the right

---

[25] See para 7(2) of Schedule 5, Scotland Act 1998.
[26] GA Resn 217A(III), UN Doc A/810 at 71 (1948) as a General Assembly Resolution was not a legally binding instrument but was rather designed to be a 'common standard of achievement for all peoples of all nations': Eleanor Roosevelt, US representative to the UN and Chairperson of the United Nations Committee on Human Rights. The Declaration embraces a wide spectrum of rights and freedoms, civil and political, social, cultural and economic and some if not all of the rights and freedoms guaranteed would today be regarded as having achieved the status of customary international law.
[27] UKTS 6 (1977) Cmnd 6702. Entered into force March 1976.
[28] Ibid. Entered into force January 1976.
[29] UKTS 77 (1969), Cmnd 4108. Entered into force 1969.
[30] Misc 1 (1982), Cmnd 8444.
[31] Misc 12 (1985), Cmnd 9593. Entered into force 1987. Note that torture is now regarded as being contrary to customary international law, '[al]though there is no universal agreement as to the precise extent of the "human rights and fundamental freedoms" guaranteed to all . . . there is at present no dissent from the view that the guarantees include, at a bare minimum, the right to be free from torture. This prohibition has become part of international law . . .'. Article 3 of the European Convention on the Protection of Human Rights and Fundamental Freedoms provides 'No one shall be subjected to torture, inhuman or degrading treatment or punishment.' See also European Convention for the Prevention of Torture and Inhuman or Degrading Treatment or Punishment 1987.
[32] 28 ILM 1448.
[33] Article 1.1.

to work, which includes the right of everyone to the opportunity to gain his living by work which he freely chooses or accepts ...'.[34] 'It recognises right of everyone to the enjoyment of just and favourable conditions of work which ensure, in particular:

(a) remuneration which provides all workers, as a minimum with:
   (i) fair wages and equal remuneration for work of equal value without distinction of any kind, in particular women being guaranteed conditions of work not inferior to those enjoyed by men, with equal pay for equal work;
   (ii) a decent living for themselves and their families ... ;
(b) safe and healthy working conditions;
(c) equal opportunity for everyone to be promoted in his employment to an appropriate higher level, subject to no considerations other than those of seniority and competence;
(d) rest, leisure and reasonable limitation of working hours and periodic holidays with pay, as well as remuneration for public holidays.'[35]

Under the Covenant Contracting Parties are not only required to eliminate discriminatory behaviour which is adverse. Also guaranteed are the right to form and join a trade union,[36] the right of everyone to social security including social insurance,[37] an adequate standard of living,[38] the right to the enjoyment of the highest attainable standard of physical and mental health[39] and education, including higher education, which is to be made equally accessible to all on the basis of capacity, by every appropriate means, and in particular by the progressive introduction of free education.[40]

Under the Convention on the Elimination of All Forms of Discrimination Against Women Contracting Parties are required to condemn and eliminate discriminatory behaviour and to this end must, for example, adopt appropriate legislative and other measures, including sanctions where appropriate, prohibiting all discrimination against women.[41] The Convention on the Rights of the Child imposes wide-ranging obligations on Contracting Parties in which 'the best interests of the child' shall at all times 'be a primary consideration'.[42]

The responsibility of the Scottish Parliament with regard to international obligations is only for those areas which fall within the Parliament's legislative competence. However, the range of the international responsibilities and obligations cited above serves to illustrate that it is inevitable that matters falling within the Parliament's legislative remit will raise issues which are the subject of international obligations. Legislative competence lies for instance in the areas of health, education, social work and housing. The rights spelt out in the Covenant on Economic, Social and Cultural Rights impinge upon all of these areas, as do

---

[34] Article 6.1.
[35] Article 7.
[36] Article 8.
[37] Article 9.
[38] Article 11.
[39] Article 12.
[40] Article 13.
[41] Article 2(b).
[42] Article 3.

pertinent provisions in other international instruments. For instance, Article 13 of the aforementioned Covenant recognises 'the right of everyone to education', but this right to education, as far as women are concerned, is further spelt out in Article 10 of the 1979 Convention on the Elimination of All Forms of Discrimination against Women[43] which calls upon Contracting Parties

> 'to take all appropriate measures to eliminate discrimination against women in order to ensure to them equal rights with men in the field of education.'

These provisions only constitute the skeleton and there now exists much more flesh on the bones, eg General Recommendations by the Committee on the Elimination of Discrimination against Women (CEDAW).[44] The Committee established under the Convention against Torture and Other Cruel, Inhuman or Degrading Treatment or Punishment has issued a number of communications relating to alleged violations of the Conventions by Contracting Parties.[45] A familiarity with the opinions of the Committee is necessary if the Convention is to be a dynamic living instrument. The Committee on the Elimination of Racial Discrimination established in accordance with Article 8 of the 1966 Convention on the Elimination of All Forms of Racial Discrimination[46] has issued a number of General Recommendations pertaining to the Convention's application.[47] It would be naïve to think that mere knowledge of the obligations spelt out in an international instrument will be sufficient to honour international obligations. More than a passing acquaintance is demanded. There now exists a tightly woven network of relevant 'soft' law which requires a holistic approach to international human rights obligations and the instruments in which they are enshrined—these instruments cannot be viewed in isolation.

The government of the United Kingdom is answerable and will remain answerable for internal compliance with international human rights obligations in spite of a possible change in the locus of responsibility for implementation. Such a division of responsibility does not raise problems if the political complexion of the relevant internal body mirrors that of the central body. However, if this is not the case there is the potential for tension. That tension would be evident in post-devolution Britain if, for example, the Scottish Parliament were to seek to implement international obligations by way of a legislative measure unacceptable to Westminster.

---

[43] GA Res 34/180, UN Doc A/34/46.
[44] The Committee was established in 1982 in accordance with Article 17 of the Convention for 'the purpose of considering the progress made in the implementation of the . . . Convention.' General Recommendations can be on either procedural matters, eg General Recommendation No 2 (Concerning Initial Reports as Submitted by State Parties), or on substantive matters such as General Recommendations Nos 12 and 19 (Violence against Women). To date the Committee has issued some 23 General Recommendations.
[45] The Committee was established under Art 17 and is competent under Art 22 to receive and consider communications from or on behalf of individuals. Acceptance by Contracting Parties of Art 22 is optional.
[46] UNTS No 195; UKTS 77 (1969), Cmnd 4108.
[47] Eg (CERD) General Recommendation XIV (42nd Session, 1994), Art 1, para 1 of the Convention; (CERD) General Recommendation XX (48th Session, 1996), Art 5 and (CERD) General Recommendation XIII (42nd Session, 1993), the training of law enforcement officials in the protection of human rights.

The situation being postulated is the use by the Secretary of State at Westminster of his power under section 58(1) to direct the Scottish Executive to refrain from the introduction of a Bill in the Scottish Parliament whose purpose is the implementation of international obligations. Such action by the Secretary of State could stem from party political differences. Conversely, the Scottish Parliament may refrain from or refuse to promulgate the appropriate legislation and in such an instance the Secretary of State may order the Scottish Executive to introduce a Bill for that purpose. It would of course remain open to the Scottish Parliament to vote down such a Bill. Not a recipe for harmonious relations!

The wording of the Scotland Act suggests a somewhat adversarial approach. Is this the best way forward?

Across the Atlantic the Canadians have adopted a more constructive model based on consultation. The Federal Government engages in dialogue with the provinces on issues relating to the conclusion of a treaty and its internal implementation. The advantage of such a consultative process is that it provides an opportunity for account to be taken of the provinces' wishes or views in respect of treaties, the subject-matter of which falls within their legislative responsibility. The consultation process is not prescribed and may take a variety of forms, eg direct discussion. Consultation may occur prior to or during negotiations on a proposed international agreement and also continues subsequent to the signing of the treaty. This is particularly necessary if implementation demands federal–provincial co-operation. Although this process of consultation has proved successful with respect to ratification and implementation of Canadian treaty obligations it has been recognised that other techniques providing more extensive co-operation may be employed. The most notable mechanisms for enhancing the consultation process are indemnity agreements, ad hoc covering agreements and *accords cadres* (general framework agreements).

The so-called indemnity agreement is required when the Federal Government concludes a treaty with a foreign power on a subject-matter which is within the competence of a provincial government. The Federal Government and the relevant province conclude an indemnity agreement according to which the province undertakes to initiate the legislation required to give effect within its territory to the obligations assumed under the relevant treaty. In addition, should the province fail to implement internally any of the obligations assumed by the Federal Government it undertakes to indemnify the Federal Government in respect of any consequent liability that might occur.

Ad hoc covering agreements are utilised to provide provincial governments with a voice in international matters affecting their interests. Normally such agreements take the form of an exchange of notes between the Canadian Federal Government and the relevant foreign power consenting to arrangements between the provincial authorities and the foreign power. Such a note gives international legal effect to the arrangements between the provincial authority and the foreign power but does not extend international rights and obligations to the provincial government. The Federal Government remains *exclusively* responsible on the international stage but the provincial body participates through co-operation with the federal authorities in the treaty-making process. Akin to the ad hoc covering agreements are *accords cadres* (general framework agreements). They are distinct from ad hoc covering agreements in that they have a wider application and afford provinces the opportunity for future agreement with the foreign power in a specific field of activity– eg education or cultural affairs.[48] The Canadian Federal Government retains international responsibility.[49]

In Australia the emphasis is also on consultation and in 1996 a revised set[50] of principles and procedures for Commonwealth State consultation on treaties was established to take account of government treaty-making reforms introduced earlier that year. The principles and procedures relate to those treaties of 'sensitivity and importance to the States and Territories' and provide that in such an instance the Commonwealth 'should, wherever practicable, seek and take into account the views of the States and the Territories in formulating Australian negotiating policy and before becoming a party to, or indicating its acceptance of, that treaty or instrument.' The Commonwealth Government is charged with the responsibility of keeping the states and territories informed of the determined policy. In instances where it is appropriate states and territories may send a representative or representatives to form part of the delegation to international conferences which are to deal with issues falling within the remit of the states and territories. The object of their inclusion is to guarantee that the states and territories are kept abreast of treaty matters and are able to articulate their position to the Commonwealth Government.

The application of the principles and procedures is subject to the caveat that they are not to be invoked to delay unnecessarily the conclusion of a treaty.

In the United Kingdom, the need for consultation was recognised in the White Paper accompanying the Scotland Bill and this has been given flesh in the form of a Memorandum and supplementary agreements made between the UK Government and the Scottish administration, which was published in October 1999. The Concordat on International Relations provides for the provision of information by the Foreign Office to the Scottish Ministers, and emphasises the need for co-operation between the respective administrations. In this respect it bears a resemblance to the Australian model discussed above.

A HUMAN RIGHTS CULTURE

The Lord Chancellor has spoken of his desire to create a human rights culture within the United Kingdom[51]:

> 'Incorporation of the Convention [the European Convention on Human Rights and Fundamental Freedoms] is going to operate as a very substantial culture change . . . . [W]e want a human rights culture to develop throughout society. And what we intend to do is to stand back and watch this bed down and monitor the success, or otherwise of the system that we have introduced and if it appears to us after that bedding period that it would be better also to have it underpinned by a human rights commission, then no doubt that is something that we will turn our attention to.'

---

[48] For instance, Cultural Agreement and Exchange of Letters between Canada and France, November 1965.
[49] For further exposition see H. Kindred (ed), *International Law Chiefly as Interpreted in Canada* (5th edn, 1993), pp 165–167.
[50] The 1996 Principles update those adopted in 1992.
[51] 'Analysis', Radio 4, 6 November 1997.

This commendable goal may be somewhat difficult to achieve given the Government's apparent reluctance to create the means for its attainment. This will be particularly true if human rights are to be seen solely within the context of the European Convention.

The creation of a human rights culture demands a change in emphasis from an increasing elaboration of rights and freedoms to implementation, viz the adoption of international human rights norms as domestic practice. This is not something which can be achieved overnight. It involves heightening awareness of human rights through the dissemination of human rights education so as to strengthen universal respect for and compliance with human rights. Effective implementation of human rights within countries demands a common understanding and awareness of human rights by all those concerned with respect for human rights—be they those who possess and seek to enforce the rights, those who are required to respect the rights or the bodies responsible for enforcement of the rights.

Creation of such a culture in Scotland demands that those within the political process be supported by access to the expertise of those conversant in international human rights. This is necessary if they are to approach human rights issues from an informed background.

The creation of a human rights culture involves a deep-bedded commitment, legal and social, to the institutions and structures on which the protection of human rights depends. What is necessary is the creation of the appropriate supporting institutional mechanism to facilitate the task of the Scottish Parliament and indeed of Westminster. The establishment of any form of human rights authority, be it national or regional, has been left open by the current Government. This is notwithstanding the 1993 United Nations General Assembly Resolution relating to the status of national institutions enjoying the competence to promote and protect human rights,[52] which endorsed the significant role that institutions at the national level can play in promoting and protecting human rights and fundamental freedoms and in developing and enhancing public awareness of those rights and freedoms.[53] The Resolution emphasised with respect to national institutions the following:

- the importance of developing, in accordance with national legislation, effective national institutions for the promotion and protection of human rights and of ensuring the pluralism of their membership and their independence;
- encouragement of member states to establish or, where they already exist, to strengthen national institutions for the promotion and protection of human rights and to incorporate those elements in national development plans; and
- encouragement of national institutions for the promotion and protection of human rights established by member states to prevent and combat all violations of human rights as enumerated in the Vienna Declaration[54] and Programme of Action and relevant international instruments.

[52] General Assembly Resolution 48/134, 20 December 1993.
[53] Ibid, Preamble.
[54] The World Conference on Human Rights was held in Vienna in June 1993. The Conference was held 45

Annexed to the Resolution are Principles Relating to the Status of National Institutions. Such institutions are to be competent to promote and protect human rights and are to be given as broad a mandate as possible. These institutions should have responsibility *inter alia* to advise government on the promotion and protection of human rights, harmonisation of national legislation and ratification of international human rights instruments.[55]

The Principles also cover the possible composition of the national institution and guarantees of its independence and pluralism and methods of operation. Additional principles concerning the status of commissions with quasi-jurisdictional competence are contained in an appendix. The Principles have subsequently been endorsed by the Council of Europe.[56]

THE APPROPRIATE INSTITUTION FOR SCOTLAND?

Currently there is no institution with a human rights remit proposed for Scotland, although that is not to say that one will not be established in the future. The Government White Paper, 'Rights Brought Home: The Human Rights Bill'[57] acknowledges this possibility but nevertheless, on the basis of financial and administrative considerations, rules out the immediate creation of a Human Rights Commission. The position of the Government appears to be to allow time for the legislation to become embedded and a human rights culture[58] to develop. Whether this is the appropriate approach is open to question because, as already highlighted, a human rights culture will not come about in a vacuum.

Two principal options have been proposed as the most appropriate institution for Scotland. They are, first, a UK body which recognises and reflects Scotland's devolved status or, second, an independent Scottish institution modelled possibly on that envisaged for Northern Ireland in the 'Good Friday Agreement'.[59] The first option is considered in some detail in a recently published report, 'A Human Rights Commission—The Options for Britain and Northern Ireland'.[60] A UK-based institution would require the appointment of a UK Commissioner to be responsible for co-ordinating the functions of Scottish, Welsh and English Commissioners. The Commissioners would have responsibilities in their respective geographical areas. The task of the Commissioner for Scotland would be that of ensuring that Scottish nuances were recognised in the implementation of international human rights obligations and that the Scottish perspective was

---

years after the adoption of the Universal Declaration of Human Rights. The text of the Vienna Declaration and the Programme of Action adopted are reproduced in 32 ILM 1661 (1993). Para 36 of the Programme of Action recognises the role of national institutions in the protection and promotion of human rights whilst affirming that states have the right to choose the type of institution perceived as the most appropriate within their own domestic context.

[55] See Principles 1, 2 and 3.
[56] 'Recommendation No R (97) 14 of the Committee of Ministers to Member States on the Establishment of Independent National Human Rights Institutions', 30 September 1997.
[57] Cm 3782.
[58] See statement of the Lord Chancellor cited above at p 32.
[59] Agreement reached at the conclusion of the all-party talks on 10 April 1998.
[60] Report written by Sarah Spencer and Ian Bynoe and published by the Institute for Public Policy Research, Autumn 1998.

reflected in the regular reports identifying the internal realisation of international obligations which Contracting Parties are required to submit under the various international Conventions.

The alternative model to a UK Commission would be a Scotland-based Commission resembling the proposed Northern Ireland body[61] but taking account of the weaknesses of the latter as identified in the report mentioned above, namely the lack of power to initiate its own litigation where there is no victim to bring the case and the absence of authority to conduct investigations into alleged human rights abuses.[62]

Whatever form of institution is created it is prerequisite that the Scottish Parliament should have access to the necessary level of advice. Such an institution would undoubtedly have a role in educating and developing a public awareness in human rights. Awareness of human rights permeating all strata of society would, it is hoped, be mirrored in policy, practice and procedures, would promote knowledge and good practice and minimise the likelihood of confrontation and litigation. The realisation of such a culture requires that the human rights institution should be at the vanguard of this process rather than fighting a rearguard action. Whatever decision is taken at Westminster regarding the creation of a Human Rights Commission it is arguable that the Scottish Parliament has the legislative competence to establish its own human rights body. This proposition is based on the Scottish Parliament's responsibility for the observance and implementation of international obligations and accordingly could establish any organ which would assist and facilitate the discharge of that function.

CONCLUSION

The Scottish Parliament has responsibility to respect a wide range of international human rights obligations and this responsibility is subject to a number of restrictions. These constraints reflect a desire on the part of the UK Government to maintain supervision of internal compliance with international obligations. As has been shown lessons can be drawn from the manner in which this is achieved in other countries. It is important that the supervision process is constructive. In relation to the European Convention Westminster has gone further in the Scotland Act 1998, in that envisaged legislation which does not comply with the Convention is outwith the legislative competence of the Scottish Parliament and legislation which falls foul of the Convention may be held unlawful by the courts. This interface of the judges with the Convention is novel and represents a new mantle on the shoulders of the judiciary. As was illustrated the European Convention is only one amongst a wide range of international instruments seeking to protect human rights. The human rights movement will be ill served if the focus is on the European Convention alone. The development of a human rights culture demands an appreciation of the full spectrum of human rights which the international community seeks to guarantee. There is a readily

---

[61] The remit of the proposed Northern Ireland Commission is spelt out in the 'Good Friday Agreement' and includes *inter alia* the provision of information and the promotion of awareness of human rights.
[62] At p 146.

perceptible need for the Scottish Parliament, the judiciary and, indeed, all those participating in the legal process to receive expert information and advice on human rights matters, particularly where international instruments have implications for devolved matters. Similarly, those responsible for determining public policy must be prepared for this new interaction with human rights law. A humans right culture will not come about without a body at the helm to chart a course through the myriad international human rights which have been affirmed in modern times. Only when the appropriate body has been established to give impetus to the development of a human rights culture can it be said with confidence that human rights are being brought home.

The authors gratefully acknowledge the research assistance of Paul Johnston.

3: THE SCOTTISH PARLIAMENT AND THE RIGHTS OF THE CHILD

Kathleen Marshall

INTRODUCTION

The thesis of this chapter is that the new Scotland needs to give a special place to the rights of its youngest citizens; and that a human rights agenda is inadequate if it fails to acknowledge the particular rights of children.

In July 1997, the Scottish Office published 'Scotland's Parliament', a White Paper paving the way for the Scotland Act 1998.[1] The Preface by the Prime Minister linked the establishment of a Scottish Parliament with the proposals to incorporate into UK law the European Convention on Human Rights. Together, these innovations would help create a new Britain, based upon decentralisation and respect for individual rights.

In the Foreword to the White Paper, the Secretary of State for Scotland promised: 'The Scottish Parliament will reflect the needs and circumstances of all the people of Scotland regardless of race, gender or disability.' No reference was made to 'age'. This is unlikely to be because there is any secret agenda to discriminate on the grounds of age; against the old or the young. It is more likely that age, if it was thought about at all, was seen to be irrelevant in the context of the new Scotland and the new human rights agenda. The Secretary of State had referred to 'all people'. Surely children are people too? The Prime Minister had referred to 'human rights'. Surely children are also human? Why should age matter?

This chapter will address:

- the relationship between 'human rights' and 'children's rights';
- the application of the European Convention on Human Rights to children;
- the contribution of the UN Convention on the Rights of the Child to a modern human rights agenda;
- the Government's responsibilities with regard to the UN Convention; and
- what needs to be done to ensure that the rights of children are respected in the new Scotland.

HUMAN RIGHTS AND CHILDREN'S RIGHTS

Children are not just people; they are 'people plus'. They are people with special vulnerabilities and particular disabilities. They are vulnerable to neglect, abuse and exploitation. They are disabled through lack of physical, economic or political power. The impact of their vulnerability is compounded by their disability.

---

[1] 'Scotland's Parliament' The Scottish Office (The Stationery Office, Edinburgh, 1997).

Children are not only likely to suffer more than adults; they are less likely than adults to be able to do anything about it.

As people, children are entitled to the whole range of human rights. As 'people plus' they need special rights in recognition of their vulnerability, and in compensation for their disability.

The humanity of children has been recognised by the international community. The major human rights documents, such as the Universal Declaration of Human Rights and the European Convention on Human Rights, apply to them as they apply to adults.

The vulnerability and disability of children have also been the subject of international attention. Children's vulnerability has been recognised by the international community since 1924 when the first Declaration of the Rights of the Child was passed by the League of Nations. Successive declarations by the United Nations in 1948 and 1959 have extended these rights from those necessary for survival to those necessary for development, and latterly to those conducive to 'happiness, love and understanding'.

Children's disability was not addressed until 1989 when the UN Convention on the Rights of the Child proclaimed the right of children to be heard and to participate in decisions on matters affecting them. It did not give children the right to *make* decisions. It said that, when children were capable of forming a view, they were entitled to express that view on any matter affecting them. The views of the child were to be taken into account in accordance with the child's age and understanding. The implications of this for the Scottish Parliament are explored further below.

Problems arise where there is an imbalance of power in the application of these international instruments. The European Convention on Human Rights has a Commission, a Court and a Committee of Ministers behind it. The Human Rights Act 1998 has now given it a more integral and powerful place within UK law. The UN Convention on the Rights of the Child is supported by a monitoring rather than an enforcement mechanism at international level, and lacks a secure place within the law. The status of the UN Convention with regard to the European Convention replicates the vulnerability and disability of the child in face of the power of the adult.

The Scottish Parliament will be required in its law-making to take full account of the European Convention on Human Rights. However, the Government has recognised that Scottish law with regard to children rests upon two pillars of rights: the European Convention on Human Rights, and the UN Convention on the Rights of the Child.

Lord Clyde's report on the Orkney Inquiry[2] had set out as recommendation number 1:

'1. Reform in the field of child law and in particular in matters of child protection should proceed under reference to the European Convention on Human Rights and the UN Convention on the Rights of the Child.'

This approach was accepted in the White Paper 'Scotland's Children' which preceded the Children (Scotland) Act 1995.[3] It is important that this twin approach is reflected in the policy-making procedures of the Scottish Parliament.

---

[2] 'The Report of the Inquiry into the Removal of Children from Orkney in February 1991' (HMSO, Edinburgh, 1992).
[3] 'Scotland's Children: Proposals for Child Care Policy and Law', The Scottish Office (HMSO, Edinburgh, 1993) para 5.16.

THE APPLICATION OF THE EUROPEAN CONVENTION ON HUMAN RIGHTS TO CHILDREN

The context for the formulation of the European Convention was the suffering of war associated with gross abrogation of human rights and fundamental freedoms. This alerted the international community to the need to set standards for the protection of individuals, sometimes against their own communities and governments. In 1945, at the close of the Second World War, the Charter of the United Nations was promulgated with the following opening words:

> 'We the peoples of the United Nations determined:
> to save succeeding generations from the scourge of war, which twice in our lifetime has brought untold sorrow to mankind, and
> to reaffirm faith in fundamental human rights, in the dignity and worth of the human person, in the equal rights of men and women and of nations large and small . . .
> Have resolved to combine our efforts to accomplish these ends.'

Three years later, the United Nations passed the Universal Declaration of Human Rights. This referred to the 'equal and inalienable rights of all members of the human family,' and the 'barbarous acts which have outraged the conscience of mankind' as a result of disregard of or contempt for human rights.

The European Convention on Human Rights followed in 1950. Its stated aim (set out in the preamble) was 'to take the first steps for the collective enforcement of certain of the rights stated in the Universal Declaration'. It was concerned with the right to life; the prohibition of slavery and torture; the right to due process of law, and freedoms of expression, thought, conscience and religion. The rights apply to 'everyone' (Article 1). Therefore they apply also to children.

The European Convention is concerned about the protection of individuals. It does not specifically address the protection of children. It assumes that children are best protected by protecting their parents or guardians and by legislating for respect for family and private life (Article 8).

Children, or adults acting on their behalf, have used the European Convention to good effect. A famous Scottish case, *Campbell and Cosans v United Kingdom*[4] in 1982, led to the abolition of corporal punishment in schools. However, the case was initiated by the parents and based upon their right to have their children educated in accordance with their own philosophical and religious convictions, rather than on the right of the child with regard to corporal punishment.

Children themselves have not often taken matters to the European Commission or Court, although they are entitled to do so. Clements, when discussing the European Convention's provision about the detention of minors for the purposes of education, commented:

> 'In view of the potentially wide scope of this provision it is perhaps surprising that it has been invoked in so few complaints, although the difficulty children have in getting direct access to legal representation may well

---

[4] *Campbell and Cosans v United Kingdom* Series A, No 48; Judgment of 25 February 1982; (1982) 4 EHRR 293.

be the explanation. The Court has also shown a propensity to treat children as objects of concern rather than individuals in their own right.'[5]

There are signs of improvement. In a more recent case, *A v United Kingdom*,[6] the complainant was a 14-year-old English boy who raised an action in respect of severe physical punishment by his stepfather when he was nine years old. The Court unanimously held that there had been a violation of Article 3 of the Convention which prohibits 'torture or inhuman or degrading treatment or punishment'. The UK Government has now accepted that the law on physical chastisement needs to be changed.

However, the European Convention can also have unfortunate implications for children. Its emphasis on parental rights, combined with its great power with regard to enforcement relative to the UN Convention, means that there is a temptation for the Government to go for a 'quick fix' to avoid embarrassment in the European arena, rather than adopt a more balanced approach which takes full account of the rights of children.

This was the situation with regard to the Government's response to the case of *McMichael v United Kingdom*.[7] The European Court of Human Rights upheld complaints by the applicant parents alleging breaches of Articles 6.1 and 8 of the Convention in respect that they had been denied access to some of the reports which had formed the basis of a decision by the children's hearing to remove their child from their care. Article 6.1 protects the right to a fair trial, whereas Article 8 safeguards respect for family and private life.

Whilst few would disagree with the principle that parents should have access to these documents, there has been considerable concern amongst those involved in child protection about the manner in which the European Court's decision was translated into Scottish law. A speedy amendment was made to the rules governing the children's hearing system to require that parents must be provided with all of the information given to the children's panel members who constitute the children's hearing. Unlike other legal provisions about access to information, no exceptions were allowed.

In particular, there was considerable concern that the new provision reduced the opportunities for children and young people themselves to present their views in writing to the children's hearing. Despite the relative informality of the proceedings, it is known that some children and young people find it difficult to speak out. It is also known that they are often reluctant to express concerns or fears about their parents' care for them, if their parents are present or if they think their parents will find out what they have said. A practice had developed whereby children and young people had been encouraged and assisted to write their views down in a way that would alert the hearing to their concerns and provide a potential basis for questions and discussion. Anecdotal evidence from Children's Reporters within the hearing system suggests that, since the rules were changed, some young people have had to be reminded that parents will have access to their

---

[5] L Clements, *European Human Rights: Taking a Case Under the Convention* (Sweet & Maxwell, London, 1994) p 129.
[6] *A v United Kingdom* Judgment delivered by the European Court of Human Rights, 23 September 1998; 5 BHRC 137.
[7] *McMichael v United Kingdom* Series A, No 308; Judgment of 24 February 1995; (1995) 20 EHRR 205.

reports so that they can consider amending them to take account of that development. This contravenes the young person's right to express his or her views freely, and also reduces the quality of information available to the hearing to enable them to make a decision in that young person's best interests. Thus, the practical implementation of the European Court's decision has resulted in abrogation of the rights of children under the UN Convention.

It is questionable whether such an all-embracing response was necessary to fulfil the requirements of the Convention. The European Commission's published opinion on the *McMichael* case had observed:

> 'The Commission is not called upon to consider whether there are reports or other documents which may contain material which should not be disclosed to parents either because it is detrimental to the child or to their own interests. It has not been alleged in this case that there were any special reasons for withholding the reports from the applicants.'

At the time of writing, it is understood that consideration is being given to amending the law to safeguard the rights of children and young people in this respect.

The Council of Europe, author of the European Convention on Human Rights, has itself recognised a need to acknowledge the principles of the UN Convention on the Rights of the Child. To this end it drafted a Convention on the Exercise of Children's Rights, purportedly based on the principles of the UN Convention. It was opened for signature and ratification in 1996. However, it is a weak document which does little to advance the rights of children and arguably waters down the principles of the UN Convention.[8] There has been very little positive response from member states to it.

The relevance for the Scottish Parliament is that the increased legal significance of the European Convention on Human Rights in domestic law needs to be balanced by a higher profile for the UN Convention on the Rights of the Child within the government of the new Scotland.

THE CONTRIBUTION OF THE UN CONVENTION ON THE RIGHTS OF THE CHILD TO A MODERN HUMAN RIGHTS AGENDA

The context of the drafting of the UN Convention was quite different from that of the European Convention. Detrick[9] sets it against the debates in the 1960s and 70s about the 'rights of the child' and how these related to the rights of those caring for them. It was estimated that 80 international instruments already included some aspects of children's rights.[10] There was some debate about whether a special Convention on children was necessary or desirable. However, Detrick sets out a number of justifications for a Convention dealing with children[11]:

---

[8] For a discussion of this Convention, see K Marshall, *Children's Rights in the Balance: The Participation –Protection Debate* (The Stationery Office, Edinburgh, 1997) ch 4.
[9] S Detrick (ed), *The United Nations Convention on the Rights of the Child—A Guide to the 'Travaux Préparatoires'* (Martinus Nijhoff, Dordrecht, 1991).
[10] Ibid, p 20.
[11] Ibid, p 29.

- It had been recognised since 1924 that children were particularly vulnerable and had specific needs.
- Existing human rights instruments, which were of universal application, had not been drawn up with children in mind. They were scattered throughout a large number of documents and therefore contained some inconsistencies. They did not reflect current knowledge and experience with regard to children's issues.
- Respect for rights is dependent on awareness of them. Current provisions regarding children were too disparate. A comprehensive Convention would help increase awareness and lead to effective action.
- Countries which had not ratified other international Conventions, which contained some provisions relating to children, might be prepared to ratify a Convention focusing on children alone.

In short, there was a need to translate the recognition of children's vulnerability into a focused and up-to-date instrument which would raise awareness of children's issues and encourage states to take effective action to address them.

The impetus for the Convention was the 1979 International Year of the Child. A working group was established to draft the Convention. It took 10 years to produce a document which could be accepted as providing a base line for the rights of children across the globe. This careful and lengthy preparation paid off. The Convention was passed by the UN General Assembly on 20 November 1989, and opened for ratification. It has become the fastest and most extensively ratified Convention in the history in international relations. At the time of writing, all but two states have ratified the Convention. The missing two are the USA (who are actively considering it) and Somalia.

Implementation of the Convention is monitored by a Committee on the Rights of the Child established by the United Nations. States are obliged to submit a progress report on implementation two years after ratification, and every five years thereafter. Unlike the European Convention on Human Rights, there is no international court or proper enforcement procedure. To that extent, it is a weaker instrument than the European Convention. The implications for children in Scotland, and indeed for the rest of the United Kingdom, have been discussed above.

In terms of content, the UN Convention reiterates the need to protect the family which, its preamble proclaims, is the 'fundamental group of society and the natural environment for the growth and the well-being of all its members and particularly children'. However, it also recognises that, just as individuals sometimes need protection from the state (the European Convention's angle), so children sometimes need protection from their families (Articles 9 and 19 of the UN Convention).

There is an element here of the microcosm reflecting the concerns of the macrocosm. In the political arena, the insight is often repeated that 'Power tends to corrupt. Absolute power tends to corrupt absolutely.' Care involves power, and power is susceptible to abuse. Children with no power to counter or qualify the power of adults will tend to be the object of corruption.

The UN Convention defines 'child' as anyone under the age of 18. The focus on child protection, and the inadequacies in that respect of the European Convention, tend to concentrate attention on the lower end of the age scale. However, there are other justifications for supplementing the European Convention with one focusing particularly on children and young people.

The Universal Declaration of Human Rights had declared that:

> 'It is essential, if man is not to be compelled to have recourse, as a last resort, to rebellion against tyranny and oppression, that human rights should be protected by the rule of law.'

Much is said today about the alienation of young people, their lack of interest in politics and government and their aversion to authority. If the new Scotland and its modern human rights agenda do not respect the rights of young people and give them a voice, then we leave them no choice but to resort to action to speak where their words cannot be heard. To paraphrase the Universal Declaration: It is essential, if young people are not to be compelled to have recourse, as a last resort, to rebellion against a system that does not listen to them, that their rights to be heard and respected be built into the fabric of the new Scotland.

Two of the basic principles of the UN Convention address these issues. Article 3 addresses the primacy of the interest of children in all actions that concern them. Article 12 gives children a right to be heard, and to have their view taken into account on matters affecting them. The Convention carefully balances the right of children to have their best interests given a high priority with the right to make an effective and appropriate contribution to decision-making.

These rights do not refer solely to matters that affect them individually, but also to matters affecting them as a group, such as the running of schools, and to matters of state. The following section of this chapter explores the Government's responsibilities with regard to these two basic principles.

GOVERNMENTAL RESPONSIBILITIES WITH REGARD TO THE UN CONVENTION ON THE RIGHTS OF THE CHILD

Articles 3 and 12 of the UN Convention on the Rights of the Child represent basic principles which need to be built into the fabric of parliamentary processes if they are to be properly respected. The responsibility of governments to ensure that this happens has been the subject of much comment by the UN Committee on the Rights of the Child.

Article 3 states:

> '1. In all actions concerning children, whether undertaken by public or private social welfare institutions, courts of law, administrative authorities or legislative bodies, the best interests of the child shall be a primary consideration.'

It should be noted that 'legislative bodies' are listed amongst those required to take account of the child's best interests.

In its 'Guidelines for Periodic Reports' the UN Committee on the Rights of the Child said that:

'33. Reports should indicate whether the principle of the best interests of the child and the need for it to be a primary consideration in all actions concerning children is reflected in the Constitution and relevant national legislation and regulations.'[12]

Some countries have already written the rights of the child into their constitutions. Colombia's constitution says 'The rights of children take precedence over the rights of other persons.'[13] It must be said, however, that there is concern about what impact these statements have upon practice; something which cannot be assumed.

When considering the United Kingdom's initial report to it, the Committee suggested that:

'[T]he general principles of the Convention, particularly the provisions of its article 3, relating to the best interests of the child, should guide the determination of policy-making at both the central and local levels of government.'[14]

Nigeria[15] and Hong Kong[16] were criticised for not having governmental procedures which ensured that the best interests of the child guided their decision-making processes. It was suggested that a child impact analysis accompany policy proposals.

France was commended for its annual report to the Parliamentary Assemblies on the implementation of the Convention, which was seen as a contribution towards keeping the interests of children on the parliamentary agenda.[17]

The principle is not restricted to policy considerations, but applies also to the allocation of resources. This point has often been expressed strongly by the UN Committee. For example, it told the French delegates that the: 'best interests of the child . . . apply irrespective of budgetary resources.'[18] The same point was made to Paraguay.[19]

From this one might conclude that:

- Legislative bodies must take the child's best interests as a primary consideration in *all* actions which concern children.
- There is encouragement to reflect the principle of the child's best interests in the constitution.
- Procedures should be set up to ensure that the best interests of children guide the government's decision-making process.
- The principle applies also to the allocation of resources by governments.

---

[12] 'General Guidelines Regarding the Form and Contents of Periodic Reports to be Submitted by States Parties Under Article 44, Paragraph 1(B) of the Convention, Adopted by the Committee on the Rights of the Child at its 343rd meeting (thirteenth session) on 11 October 1996' quoted in R Hodgkin and P Newell, *Implementation Handbook for the Convention on the Rights of the Child* (UNICEF, New York, 1998).
[13] *Implementation Handbook* op cit, p 43.
[14] UN Document UK IRCO Add 34 para 24, quoted in *Implementation Handbook* op cit, p 41.
[15] *Implementation Handbook* op cit, p 42.
[16] Ibid.
[17] Ibid, p 43.
[18] Ibid, p 41.
[19] Ibid, p 41.

Article 12 of the UN Convention says:

> '1. States Parties shall assure to the child who is capable of forming his or her own views, the right to express those views freely in all matters affecting the child, the views of the child being given due weight in accordance with the age and maturity of the child.'

It should be noted that this article applies to 'all matters affecting the child'. Does that mean matters affecting the child personally and directly, or does it include more general matters such as those that might be the subject of debate in a Scottish Parliament?

A common-sense reading would be that the 'all' in the article applies to all matters, general or specific to the child concerned. It is significant that, when the Convention was being drafted, there was at one point a list of specific matters attached to the Article 12 right, restricting it to matters 'concerning his own person' including 'marriage, choice of occupation, medical treatment, education and recreation'. A decision was made to delete this list and give the right a more general application. This is reflected in the 'Guidelines for Periodic Reports' in which the UN Committee asked states submitting reports:

> '45. Please provide information on any bodies or instances where the child has the right to participate in decision-making, such as schools or local councils . . .
>
> 47. Please indicate how the views of the child obtained through public opinion, consultations and assessment of complaints are taken into consideration in the legal provisions, and in policy or judicial decisions.'[20]

Comments on Hong Kong's Initial Report referred to 'children's participation in the family, school and society'.[21] And indeed the response to the United Kingdom's report suggested that: 'the State Party consider the possibility of further mechanisms to facilitate the participation of children in decisions affecting them, including within the family and the community.'[22]

The Committee has welcomed initiatives in countries which have set up children's or youth parliaments out of respect for Article 12 and has approved of and encouraged attempts by states to involve children themselves in the process of implementing the Convention.

The conclusion is that Article 12 has relevance, not only when decisions are being made which affect a child personally, but also when decisions are being made that are of concern to children as a group. Children's views and experiences must inform policy-making.

There is also a practical point to all of this; it is not merely 'political correctness' in the derogatory sense of the term. One of the insights of the drafters of the Convention, which informed their approach to children's views, was that it makes no sense to assert that you have made a decision in the interests of children, if

---

[20] *Implentation Handbook* op cit, p 607.
[21] Ibid, p 152.
[22] Ibid, p 152.

children have views on the matter and you do not know what they are. Taking account of the views of children is an essential element of determining where children's interests lie. Failure to do so can lead to policies which 'miss the mark' and waste resources. In his Foreword to the White Paper the then Secretary of State for Scotland, Donald Dewar, said of the Scottish Parliament:

> 'This reform will not in itself solve the problem of resources or banish the dilemmas of government. What it can do is connect and involve people with the decisions that matter to them. It can bring a sense of ownership to political debate and a new confidence to our affairs.'

It is to be hoped that children are included in this insight.

International law requires us to ensure that the new Scottish Parliament is guided by its commitment to the best interests of children and is informed in its decisions by their views. It would have been nice to have had this stated up front in the White Paper. Apart from anything else, it would have impressed the UN Committee. It would seem perverse to neglect these international commitments when devising a new parliamentary system.

RESPECTING THE RIGHTS OF CHILDREN IN THE NEW SCOTLAND

Children and young people do not have a vote. Their voices and their needs are too easily ignored. If the rights of children are to be fully respected, it is essential that the adult-centred perspective of the European Convention on Human Rights is balanced by the child-centred approach of the UN Convention on the Rights of the Child. The Scottish Parliament must make its decisions with the interests of children as a primary consideration, and informed by their views.

This means we must:

1. ensure that the Scottish Parliament takes full account of the principles of the UN Convention as well as the European Convention;
2. ensure that mechanisms exist to identify matters that concern children;
3. ensure that decisions on these matters reflect the primary consideration of the best interests of children;
4. ensure that mechanisms exist to ascertain the views of children; and
5. ensure that the views of children are weighed in the balance appropriately when decisions are being made which affect them.

1. Ensure that the Scottish Parliament takes full account of the UN Convention

The most satisfactory way to do this would have been for the Scotland Act itself to include a reference to the UN Convention on the Rights of the Child.

In 1998 a grouping of interested agencies and individuals initiated a campaign under the banner 'Scotland for Children' with the aim of securing 'a commitment to children at the heart of Scotland's Parliament'.[23] It was noted that the Human

---

[23] 'Scotland for Children' campaign leaflet (Save the Children, Scotland, 1998).

Rights Bill, which formed the basis of the 1998 Act, contained a clause requiring Ministers of the UK Parliament to make a statement about the extent of compatibility of any Bill with the European Convention on Human Rights. The Scotland Bill, which was also before Parliament at that time, required a member of the Scottish Executive in charge of a Bill to make a statement to Parliament about its legislative competence. Using these as a starting point, the Scotland for Children Campaign drafted a clause for the Scotland Bill, requiring a member of the Scottish Executive to make a statement to the effect that a Bill was compatible with the UN Convention on the Rights of the Child. The clause was tabled with all-party support. However it was crowded out of the discussion by the clamour of other voices and failed to stimulate any real debate.

The conclusion to be drawn from this failure is that the message has not got through to policy makers that this is a real issue with real implications for real children. A sustained effort is required to get this matter onto the agenda.

2. Ensure that mechanisms exist to identify matters that concern children

The appointment in 1997 of a Minister for Children's Issues within the Scottish Office was greeted with approval by agencies with an interest in the needs and rights of children. There was some dismay that children's issues formed only a small part of the portfolio of Mr Sam Galbraith, who was appointed to the post. Nevertheless, he quickly announced a 'child-proofing' policy for all Scottish Executive departments. This requires departments to think about the effects on children when developing policy. It is not as comprehensive an approach as the requirement for a 'child impact analysis' would be. This would require departments not only to 'think about' the potential effects on children, but to commit those thoughts to paper in a way that would allow them to be held to account for their conclusions.

The 'child-proofing' strategy is a welcome start. However, it would be more helpful were Scottish Executive departments required to attach a 'child impact analysis' to all policy proposals, and particularly to any Bills for presentation to the Scottish Parliament.

There are other possibilities for ensuring that the interests and views of children and young people are taken into account appropriately. There has been substantial support within Scotland, and indeed the rest of the United Kingdom, for the appointment of a commissioner or ombudsman for children whose functions would complement that of the Minister. At the very least, an annual report to the Scottish Parliament on the state of Scotland's children would provide a useful focus for the ingathering of information and an invaluable pointer to the way ahead.

3. Ensure that decisions on these matters reflect the primary consideration of the best interests of children

Even if we had a bold and high-profile statement about the place of children's interests in the considerations of the Scottish Parliament, and even if we had a mechanism for identifying where the interests of Scottish children lay, we would still need mechanisms for feeding those insights into the policy-making process and ensuring they were given appropriate weight.

The interests of children must be represented at the highest level of the Scottish Executive through their Minister. The Minister and his staff must brief the Secretary of State for Scotland when he represents Scottish interests at UK level on the reserved matters which are clearly important for Scottish children.

In particular, relationships with international bodies such as the United Nations and European bodies must take full account of the Scottish situation. The United Kingdom's first report to the UN Committee on the Rights of the Child was a prime example of the marginalisation of Scotland's children. There was little informed input from Scotland. Information presented as being of UK application often excluded the Scottish dimension, which at times was significantly different. Whilst the Second Report shows some limited improvement, it cannot be said that it adequately represents the position of Scottish children in all relevant matters. We must ensure that the existence of the Scottish Parliament and the Scottish Executive produces particular Scottish perspectives which help avoid rather than exaggerate this tendency towards marginalisation at international level.

4. Ensure that mechanisms exist to ascertain the views of children

There are various initiatives underway at the moment attempting to further the participation of children at all levels of society through emerging organisations such as 'Article 12', 'Connect Youth' and the Youth Parliament initiative.

There is also a group working to establish an International Children's Parliament in Edinburgh, the aim of which is to go beyond the 'talking shop' and bring children together to address specific topics in creative ways and to communicate with other children at home and abroad through information technology.

We can be creative. Just as there is no need for the Scottish Parliament to be a mini carbon copy of the UK one, so there is no need for children's participation to be channelled only through mechanisms devised to suit adult needs. Some children and young people will want to debate in a formal way and this should be encouraged, but an innovative Scottish Parliament setting out to fulfil its international obligations towards children and to make better decisions by involving them in the process, can look for innovative ways to achieve this end.

This is also where the Scottish Parliament's responsibilities for local government are of interest. Already in some local authority areas, interesting experiments in child and youth participation are being carried out. These should be supported and monitored both because they are useful in themselves in facilitating local participation, and because they can provide a bottom-up base and model for participation at a national level.

Help is also available from international models. In France, for example, children's and young people's councils exist at various levels. A detailed study of them was completed in 1993.

5. Ensure that the views of children are weighed in the balance appropriately when decisions are being made which affect them

It is a waste of time and resources to do all this if we do not intend taking children's views seriously. Where they are taken seriously, it increases their respect for authority and their ownership of policy; both of which are aims consistent with government policy.

It was impressive, during the evidence-taking sessions leading up to the Children (Scotland) Act 1995, to watch the Special Standing Committee appointed to consider the Bill listen intently to the views of the young people from Who Cares? Scotland (a campaigning and advocacy organisation for young people with experience of the care system) and to see the seriousness with which they took them into account. I think all present would have agreed that the young persons' contribution was invaluable. It can be done, and we should continue to try to do it.

CONCLUSION

Scotland's Parliament is likely to break new ground in many ways. It has an electoral system designed to achieve a measure at least of proportional representation. It has a fixed term of office (or more fixed than the UK Parliament). It has adopted modern methods of working. It aims to be accessible, open and responsive to the needs of the public (including children). The proposals have been influenced by the principle of 'subsidiarity'. How far down does it go? Does not the ultimate in subsidiarity involve giving children a voice in affairs which affect them?

The establishment of the Scottish Parliament is an exciting development. The laying of the foundation stones of a modern human rights agenda through the Human Rights Act 1998 is a very positive move. But it will be flawed if it fails to acknowledge the special needs and rights of those vulnerable citizens who do not have a vote.

4: INCORPORATION AND INTERPRETATION OF GUARANTEES FOR RESPECT FOR PRIVATE LIFE: A THREAT TO PRESS FREEDOM?

Jim Murdoch

Incorporation of the European Convention on Human Rights will prove to be as crucial an event for Scots law as the establishment of a Scots Parliament. Constitutional change of the magnitude proposed by the Labour Government elected in 1997 is of seismic proportions when considered alongside the usually tranquil and sluggish development of the United Kingdom. Devolution will lead to a steady stream of new Scottish legislation on a wide range of issues; and direct reliance upon the European human rights treaty by litigants seeking to question the validity of such legislation may require domestic courts to engage in qualitative assessment of underlying policy. Executive practice, too, will now be policed by the judiciary in terms of its compatibility with Convention norms. This will bring new opportunities and challenges. Experimentation in constitutional innovation will unsettle the long-established (but not necessarily delicately balanced) machinery of government.

From the perspective of the citizen, the overall result is likely to be an enhanced package of individual rights. From the European perspective, the impression will be that the United Kingdom has caught up with the constitutional development of other mature liberal democracies. Devolution of legislative authority to a regional assembly and incorporation of the European Convention on Human Rights will, after all, produce a form of governmental arrangement not dissimilar to that applying in many other European states. More particularly, litigants will be able in Scotland for the first time to rely directly upon Convention guarantees in domestic courts and in tribunals. This will not only involve taking Strasbourg jurisprudence into account in questions of statutory interpretation and in the development of the common law, but also in seeking to persuade courts that legislation or executive action violates European norms. Little of this would be seen as dramatic in other West European legal systems, and most of this would even be considered as a self-evident necessity by the emerging democracies of Central and East Europe.

In Strasbourg, the effect is likely to be, at the very least, the correction of the unfortunate impression made by the relentless stream of British applications and largely explained on the ground that British applicants currently have no option other than an international forum in which to air grievances. The Euro-euphemism is that Britain is one of Strasbourg's 'best customers'. It is not merely the quantity of adverse Court judgments concerning the United Kingdom, but more importantly their quality. British law and practice have been found wanting in such matters as basic guarantees for those deprived of their liberty; infliction of inhuman and degrading treatment; breach of the right to a fair hearing; lack of controls over telephone-tapping; censorship of prisoners' mail; interference with the freedom of the press; and even deprivation of life. Yet the vast bulk of such cases have their origins in the law and practice of other parts of the United Kingdom. Scottish applications have been relatively few in number. Certainly, Scottish applicants have successfully challenged the lack of legal aid during criminal appeals as a violation of the principle of 'equality of arms',[1] while the failure to accord parents access to documents relied upon in a children's hearing has been held to breach fair hearing and respect for family life guarantees.[2] The case to make perhaps the greatest impact upon the popular conscience in Scotland, *Campbell and Cosans v United Kingdom*,[3] indeed eventually led to the removal of corporal punishment from state schools. However, usage of the Convention in Scotland or by Scottish applicants has been minimal. Prior to incorporation, it would have been no exaggeration to suggest that the Convention's overall standing in domestic legal systems was at its weakest in Scotland.[4] The consequence is that large tracts of Scots law have remained untested and untried. The Human Rights Act 1998 and the Scotland Act 1998 will reverse this situation, and challenges based upon Convention guarantees from litigants in civil proceedings and from accused persons in criminal trials are unavoidable. From a situation in which the Convention is rarely if ever discussed, the courts will be propelled into applying Convention guarantees on a frequent basis. Much basic scrutiny of the compatibility of existing laws and practices with the Convention will be done through such challenges. Yet there is also further scope for courts and other 'public authorities' to engage in the construction of new legal rules and principles. A particular recurring theme has been the perceived judicial inability and legislative unwillingness to deal with media intrusions into privacy.[5] Now there are opportunities—or as some see it, risks—for the courts in creating real protection through an activist approach to the interpretation of Article 8's requirement to respect private and family life.[6] During parliamentary scrutiny of the Human Rights Bill in the House of Lords in particular, the question of the impact of incorporation upon press freedom was rarely far away.[7] The issue of press freedom versus privacy regulation provides much scope for balancing two competing and equally compelling values, an exercise largely avoided by previous executives and legislatures but now one which shortly will undoubtedly be laid before the judiciary. This issue provides an admirable case-study for the student of incorporation. This chapter seeks to examine current Strasbourg approaches to privacy, and then to discuss whether parliamentary concerns were well founded. Beforehand, though, some scene-setting is desirable.

---

[1] *Granger* v *UK*, 28 Mar 1990, Ser A No 174, [1990] TLR 256; *Boner* v *UK*, 28 Oct 1994, Ser A No 300-B, (1995) 19 EHRR 246; *Maxwell* v *UK*, Ser A No 300-C, (1995) 19 EHRR 97.
[2] *McMichael* v *UK*, 24 Feb 1995, Ser A No 307-B, [1995] 2 FCR 718, (1995) 20 EHRR 205.
[3] 25 Feb 1982, Ser A No 48, (1982) 4 EHRR 293.
[4] For a discussion of use made by Scottish applicants of the Convention, see Murdoch, 'Scots Law and the European Convention on Human Rights' in Dickson, *Human Rights and the European Convention* (Sweet & Maxwell, 1997) pp 113–142.
[5] See, eg Calcutt, 'Review of Press Self-Regulation', Cm 2135 (1993) at para 7.23: 'further consideration to the introduction of a new tort of privacy' urged.
[6] Cf Lord Keith's comment in *A-G* v *Guardian Newspapers (No 2)* [1990] 1 AC 109 at 255 that 'the right to personal privacy is clearly one which the law should . . . seek to protect'. See, further, Bingham, 'Should there be a Law to Protect Rights of Personal Privacy?' [1996] EHRLR 450.
[7] Eg 582 HL Deb 1230 (3 Nov 1997); 583 HL Deb 784-786 (24 Nov 1997).

THE FIRST FIFTY YEARS: THE ECHR AND SCOTS LAW

The title of the Government's White Paper on incorporation, 'Bringing Rights Home', reflects the rather paradoxical situation that while Convention guarantees reflect values embedded in British law and while British jurists were influential in the Convention's drafting, Scottish courts have subsequently proved reluctant to allow use of arguments based upon Convention guarantees. In essence, the Convention is a collection of values which infuse the common law and are shared by other liberal democracies. The substance of Convention guarantees is commonplace: equality before the law, fair hearings, impartiality of judges, no retroactive lawmaking, protection against discrimination and against wrongful deprival of liberty, recognition of the concept of marriage, freedom of conscience and respect for privacy and belief, and protection of property rights. Such ideas have been articulated and developed by the Scottish judiciary long before the Convention's ratification. Recourse to an external body of principles such as the Convention when deciding cases indeed could have been seen to restrict judicial discretion and strengthen the appearance of judicial impartiality. Refusal to allow a treaty to enter a legal system by 'the back door' in the absence of parliamentary transformation of international law into national law by means of statute confuses constitutional propriety with recognition of the Convention as an informal source of public policy. Refusal to admit discussion of the Convention also potentially impoverishes the legal system: it denies the accepted approach that '[e]quity remains a valid and unexhausted source of Scots law in that it is still open to a court to delimit a rule or principle in the light of what seems consistent with reason and natural justice'.[8] The Scottish Law Commission itself was making use of the Convention as a source of public policy in drafting recommendations for law-reform measures.[9]

Adverse rulings from Strasbourg usually require the Government to amend executive practices or to introduce proposals for law reform. The Scottish judiciary until now has been largely able to ignore the European Convention. While executive suspicion of incorporation of the Convention has explained parliamentary inaction, it has not fully justified the hostility shown by the Scottish courts towards litigants' arguments based upon Convention obligations. Ever since the two decisions of *Kaur v Lord Advocate* and *Moore v Secretary of State for Scotland* in the early 1980s, Scottish courts have been unable to have regard to the Convention as an aid to statutory interpretation or as a tool for shaping the development of the common law. Over the past two decades, Scots law has become increasingly out of line with the approach adopted in the English courts where the Convention has long been used as a source of public policy and as an aid in the interpretation of statutory ambiguities, a situation which led Lord President Hope in 1996 in *T, Petitioner*[10] to argue the need for reversal of these cases and have the Scottish courts follow English law.

The Human Rights Act 1998 and the Scotland Act 1998 reverse this situation.

---

[8] D M Walker, *The Scottish Legal System* (6th edn, W Green, 1990) p 459.
[9] Lord Hope, 'From Maastricht to the Saltmarket', Society of Solicitors in the Supreme Courts of Scotland, Biennial Lecture, 1992, at 15, citing Scottish Law Commission, 'Report on Documentary Evidence and Proof of Undisputed Facts in Criminal Evidence' (1992), para 4.17.
[10] 1997 SLT 724.

Conferring a constitutional mandate upon the domestic judiciary to ensure a general respect for Convention rights runs the risk, according to critics, of permitting the courts to engage in a new phase of judicial activism. Public authorities (including central government agencies, Scottish Executive Ministers, local government, the police, the prison service and certain privatised utilities) will be placed under a duty to act in accordance with Convention requirements which will be enforceable through judicial review or other forms of legal action in domestic courts and tribunals.[11] In interpreting any legislation (including Acts of the Scottish Parliament) judges will be directed to give a meaning as far as possible compatible with the Convention. Where it is impossible to reconcile Convention guarantees with an Act of the Westminster Parliament, higher courts may make a declaration of incompatibility.[12] This will not affect the validity of Westminster legislation, but will almost certainly prompt rapid executive and legislative action to amend the offending statute to bring it into line with Strasbourg requirements.[13] Under the Scotland Act, neither the Scottish Executive nor the Scottish Parliament will have the power to act in contravention of the Convention, and Scottish Parliamentary legislation, if successfully challenged on this ground, will be declared void.[14] Arguably, the power given to inferior courts and tribunals to refer challenges to Edinburgh legislation to the Court of Session and to the High Court of Justiciary for decision or in turn for referral to the Judicial Committee of the Privy Council will result in a higher level of domestic protection for human rights in Scotland than elsewhere in the United Kingdom. Devolved matters are more likely to raise human rights concerns than subjects to be retained by Westminster, and the net outcome should be a gain for protection of the individual.

A NEW LAW OF PRIVACY?

Scots law has only provided the minimum respect for privacy, and this is reflected in traditional approaches to the disposal of cases in which a privacy argument arises. If a law of privacy indeed exists, it does so only in a rudimentary fashion. Nor have the Scottish courts had much opportunity to shape any general approach to freedom of expression for the media—the obverse side of the question—in a way which has occurred in England.[15] If we have any legal rules

---

[11] Human Rights Act 1998, ss 6–8.
[12] Human Rights Act 1998, ss 3–5.
[13] Human Rights Act 1998, s 10.
[14] Scotland Act 1998, ss 28 and 53(2).
[15] As, for example, in *Derbyshire County Council* v *Times Newspapers Ltd* [1993] 1 All ER 1011 (HL) where the English courts refused to recognise any right on the part of a local authority to raise an action for defamation. In *Hellewell* v *Chief Constable of Derbyshire* [1995] 1 WLR 804 at 807, the court even suggested that the unauthorised photographing of an individual 'engaged in some private act' using a telephoto lens would amount to a breach of confidence as much as the publication of material taken from a lost or stolen letter or diary. Cf Application Nos 28851/95 and 28852/95, *Earl Spencer and Countess Spencer* v *United Kingdom*, decision of 16 Jan 1998, 25 EHRR CD 105, where the Commission noted (at 117-118) that there had been a 'significant clarification of the scope and extent of a breach of confidence action' and the applicants had not shown this remedy to be insufficient or ineffective.

on what constitutes privacy,[16] they are to be found, as in England and Wales, in the arenas of police powers of search and entry, and as restrictions upon freedom of expression through a handful of private law rules on such matters as trespass, copyright and (more recently) breach of confidence. In the first, the courts often favour recognition of extensions to police powers on the grounds of social policy;[17] in the second, restraints upon free speech are still patchy and uncertain,[18] and in any case in Britain most faith is placed upon media self-regulation.

How will the courts respond to the challenges posed by incorporation and by devolution? During parliamentary stages of the Human Rights Bill in the House of Lords, Lord Wakeham, the Chairman of the Press Complaints Commission, expressed concern that incorporation could have a fundamental impact upon press freedom. In reply, the Lord Chancellor suggested that any judicial development of privacy protection would be more satisfactory if it took place within the ambit of Articles 8 and 10: the judges were in any case 'pen-poised regardless of [incorporation] to develop a right to privacy to be protected by the common law', and this would be 'better law' if shaped by Convention guarantees.[19] The outcome of such concerns became section 12 of the Human Rights Act. According to this section, in deciding whether to grant any relief which could affect freedom of expression, courts are to have particular regard to the importance of this freedom; where the material in issue is 'journalistic, literary or artistic', courts are also to have regard to the extent to which the material has (or is about to) become available in the public domain, whether it would be in the public interest for the material to be published, and any relevant privacy code.[20] It is difficult to see what effect this will have in practice. The clear intent is to restrain 'pen-poised' judges.

---

[16] As opposed to references to privacy in statute: eg Broadcasting Act 1996, s 107: a task of the Broadcasting Standards Commission is 'to draw up, and from time to time review, a code giving guidance as to principles to be observed, and practices to be followed, in connection with the avoidance of . . . (b) unwarranted infringement of privacy in, or in connection with the obtaining of material included in, such programmes.' The Data Protection Act 1998 regulates the acquisition and storage of 'personal data' defined by s 1(1) as 'data which relate to a living individual'; under s 2, 'sensitive personal data' refers to information as to such matters as race or ethnic origins, political opinions, religious beliefs, sexual life, etc. However, s 32 exempts journalists from certain requirements of data protection principles, even in relation to 'sensitive personal data'.

[17] For a survey of police powers of search and surveillance, see *Stair Memorial Encyclopaedia of the Laws of Scotland*, vol 16, paras 1796–1799, and 1802–1803 (Butterworths, 1995). On occasion, the courts have taken a more rigorous line: eg *Adamson v Martin* 1916 SC 319 (destruction of impressions and photographs taken without legal authority); *Henderson v Chief Constable, Fife Police* 1988 SLT 361 (removal of bra from detainee following central government circular actionable wrong).

[18] The Calcutt Report 'Privacy and Related Matters', Cm 1102 (1992), at para 12.2, noted that 'a common law right to privacy could possibly develop in Scotland where there is a more general concept of culpa [. . . in comparison with] the more narrowly-drawn English torts'. Breach of confidence has proved to constitute an effective vessel for privacy protection where a relationship exists in which a duty of confidentiality can be presumed to exist: cf *Hellewell v Chief Constable of Derbyshire* above. See, further, Ewing and Finnie, *Civil Liberties in Scotland* (2nd edn, W. Green & Son, 1988) pp 144–160; McLean, 'Privacy, Scots Law, Human Rights, and Europe' (1996) 38 JLSS 21. For recent discussions of privacy protection in England, see Feldman, *Civil Liberties and Human Rights* (Clarendon Press, 1993) pp 353–543; and Bailey, Harris and Jones, *Civil Liberties* (4th edn, Butterworths, 1995) pp 516–577. For a sceptical view of the introduction of a law of privacy through non-ECHR means, see Bonnington, 'Privacy: Letting the Right Alone', 1992 SLT (News) 289. For further discussion of Scots law see Hogg, 'Privacy: A Valuable and Protected Interest', 1992 SLT (News) 349; and Laurie, 'Privacy, Paucity and the Press' 1993 SLT (News) 285.

[19] 583 HL Deb 784 (24 Nov 1997).

[20] Human Rights Act 1998, s 12.

Yet the section adds little if anything to the general requirement upon courts to take Strasbourg jurisprudence into account when interpreting legislation or developing the common law. It is mere window-dressing. 'Public interest' and 'any relevant privacy code' will themselves require to be interpreted in accordance with Strasbourg case-law.

In cases of press intrusion, the 'relevant privacy code' will be the Press Complaints Commission's Code of Practice[21] which purports to be (as the preamble puts it) 'the cornerstone of the system of self-regulation to which the industry has made a binding commitment', a code which is to be 'honoured not only to the letter but in the full spirit'. Clause 3 of the code provides that 'everyone is entitled to respect for his or her private and family life, home, health and correspondence', and adds that 'a publication will be expected to justify intrusions into any individual's private life without consent'. It concludes by declaring that the use of long lens photography to take pictures of people in private places (defined as 'public or private property where there is a reasonable expectation of privacy') without their consent is unacceptable. The clause—as with most other clauses which have a bearing on privacy[22]—is made subject to clause 1 which provides exceptions where these can be 'demonstrated to be in the public interest', defined as including the detection of crime, the protection of public health and safety, and 'preventing the public from being misled by some statement or action of an individual or organisation'. None of this is too far from the requirements of Articles 8 and 10. The courts will thus be bound in terms of section 12 of the Human Rights Act to consider the code, but in accordance with Convention requirements rather than any existing interpretations or judgments by the Press Complaints Commission.

In the House of Lords, the Lord Chancellor indicated his clear understanding that the Press Complaints Commission would qualify as a 'public authority' since it would meet the definition of 'any person certain of whose functions are functions of a public nature'.[23] This implies that the Commission itself would require to take Strasbourg case-law into account in adjudicating complaints, and thus new approaches and interpretations may have to be adopted. More significantly, the Lord Chancellor also acknowledged that the Commission should have primary responsibility for ensuring effective respect for privacy matters on the part of the media rather than looking to the courts to discharge this task.[24] In other words, the first line of defence for privacy would be the Commission, with the

---

[21] The current code was ratified by the PCC on 26 Nov 1997 and came into force on 1 Jan 1998. In relation to broadcasters, the relevant code would presumably be the ITC Code or the BBC's 'Producers' Guidelines' which are worded in similar terms to the PCC Code.

[22] Including clauses 4 (harassment of individuals), 6 (interviewing or photography of children), 8 (use of listening devices), and 9 (enquiries about individuals in hospitals). Cf the Broadcasting Standards Commission's Codes of Guidance (June 1998) which provides as a general principle (at para 14) that '[a]n infringement of privacy has to be justified by an *overriding* public interest in disclosure of the information. This would include revealing or detecting crime or disreputable behaviour, protecting public health or safety, exposing misleading claims made by individuals or organisations, or disclosing significant incompetence in public office. Moreover, the means of obtaining the information must be proportionate to the matter under investigation.' [Author's italics.]

[23] Human Rights Act 1998, s 6(3). For discussion on whether the PCC is open to judicial review before entry into force of the Human Rights Act, see Crown, 'Judicial Review and Press Complaints', (1997) 147 NLJ 8.

[24] 583 HL Deb 786 (24 Nov 1997).

judiciary in reserve should it not prove up to the job. This may reassure journalists concerned about 'pen-poised' judges, but only if the Commission and newspaper editors are prepared to co-operate and accept that the Human Rights Act will indeed call for enhanced respect for the private lives of individuals, section 12 notwithstanding. So far, however, the Press Complaints Commission has not been noted for its success in restraining press excesses: for some newspapers, 'public interest' may often be misinterpreted as 'of interest to the public'. The fundamental weakness of the Commission, of course, is its lack of any effective enforcement power since the remedy available to an individual whose privacy has been unfairly or inappropriately violated is at best limited. Even if the Commission were to take a robust line on protecting privacy, its restricted authority merely to require publication of its adjudication 'in full and with due prominence' is unlikely to satisfy the requirement in Article 13 of an effective remedy in domestic law for violation of Convention guarantees.[25] Whatever the effect of incorporation for the Press Complaints Commission, at some point judicial intervention is likely.

STRASBOURG PROTECTION: RESPECT FOR PRIVATE LIFE

In the absence of any domestic success in establishing a general law of privacy, faith is thus being pinned upon the potential provided by the European Convention on Human Rights. The premise is that the Human Rights Act will provide the necessary mandate for judicial creativity and for greater intervention on the part of relevant public authorities, and in particular, the Press Complaints Commission. Whether this hope is well placed or not requires some scrutiny of what the Convention requires of states, and what in turn the Human Rights Act will require of courts and public bodies. The conclusion may be that development of a new law of privacy is not strictly required by Strasbourg case-law, but on the other hand it is not precluded. The door is open for enhanced domestic protection, but any entry into this territory requires guarding against Article 10 attack.

Article 8(1) provides that 'everyone has the right to respect for his private and family life, his home and his correspondence'. These four notions are obviously closely connected.[26] The fundamental difficulty facing protagonists of the construction of a new domestic privacy law built upon the four pillars provided by Article 8—private life, family life, home and correspondence—is that Strasbourg interpretation of this guarantee seems to concentrate upon a number

---

[25] The issue whether Scots law provides 'an effective remedy before a national authority' as required by Art 13 of the Convention is an open one. Protection of privacy in Britain is perhaps essentially a case of *ubi remedium, ibi ius*—that is, the extent of privacy protection is determined by the availability of a particular remedy. The Human Rights Act does not formally incorporate Art 13 into domestic law, with the Government's justification that incorporation *per se* will be adequate to ensure that domestic law meets the requirements of Art 13. This would still be an issue for consideration by the Strasbourg Court. English law's remedy for breach of confidence seems adequate. In Application Nos 28851/95 and 28852/95, *Earl Spencer and Countess Spencer v United Kingdom*, note 15 above, the Commission accepted that breach of confidence could have provided a domestic remedy, and thus the applicants had failed to exhaust domestic remedies. For discussion of Art 13, see Harris, O'Boyle and Warbrick, *Law of the European Convention on Human Rights* (Butterworths, London, 1995) pp 443–461.
[26] Cf *Klass v Germany*, 6 Sept 1978, Ser A No 28, para 41, (1978) 2 EHRR 214: telephone conversations covered by notions of 'private life' and 'correspondence'.

of disparate topics such as sexual orientation, child care, state surveillance, prisoners' correspondence and deportation.[27] There is little established case-law in the area of 'privacy' as traditionally understood in Britain—that is, as protection from unwanted publicity. In truth, there is little guidance, even on such a basic matter as whether publication by the press of an individual's photograph would give rise to an Article 8 issue.[28] This can be explained more by the dearth of applications rather than by any fundamental refusal to recognise such claims as worthy of Article 8 discussion. It also reflects in part the comparatively recent development of positive duties assumed by states to secure 'respect', rather than simply any essentially negative duty on states to refrain from interference. Certainly, scrutiny of jurisprudence provides some understanding of the spirit in which Article 8 should be interpreted by courts and by public authorities. At the least, it does not rule out a proactive approach attempting to give protection from unwanted publicity at domestic level.

The concept of 'private life' is wide enough to cover 'the physical and moral integrity of the person, including his or her sexual life',[29] and the quality of private life as affected by the amenities of his home.[30] Issues such as educational provision,[31] corporal punishment in schools,[32] telephone-tapping,[33] data collection,[34] use of family names,[35] recognition of transsexualism,[36] and the criminalisation of homosexual conduct[37] all give rise to questions under 'private life'. These cases illustrate the scope of the protection. But Strasbourg has been unwilling to lay down any interpretation which would confine or restrict the notion of 'private life'. In its 1992 judgment in *Niemietz*, the Court declined to provide any exhaustive definition of this concept:

> '[I]t would be too restrictive to limit the notion [of "private life"] to an "inner circle" in which the individual may live his own personal life as he chooses and to exclude therefrom entirely the outside world not encompassed within that circle. Respect for private life must also comprise to a certain degree the right to establish and develop relationships with other human beings.'

Significantly, though, the Court also ruled out any distinction between private

---

[27] For surveys of Art 8 case-law, see, eg Farran, 'Recent Commission Decisions and Reports Concerning Article 8' (1996) 21 ELRev HRC/14; Feldman, 'The Developing Scope of Article 8' [1997] EHRLR 265.
[28] Cf *Friedl v Austria*, 31 Jan 1995, Ser A No 305-B, (1996) 21 EHRR 83 (case struck off the list after state agreed to destroy police photographs of demonstrators; Commission view that there was not an Art 8 violation); Application No 28122/95, *Hutcheson v United Kingdom*, dec of 27 Nov 1996, [1997] EHRLR 195 (75-ft high security tower built beside applicant's home did not constitute an Art 8 violation since the applicant had not shown she was under surveillance, and in any case, visual surveillance was within normal police duties). For a valuable discussion, see Naismith, 'Photographs, Privacy and Freedom of Expression' [1996] EHRLR 150–158.
[29] *X & Y v Netherlands*, 26 Mar 1985, Ser A No 91, para 22.
[30] *Powell & Rayner v UK*, 21 Feb 1990, Ser A No 172, para 40, [1990] TLR 142.
[31] Eg *Belgian Linguistics* case, 23 July 1968, Ser A No 6, (1968) 1 EHRR 252.
[32] Cf *Costello-Roberts v UK*, 23 Mar 1993, Ser A No 247-C, at para 36, (1995) 19 EHRR 112.
[33] Eg *Klass*, note 26 above.
[34] Eg *Lingens v Austria*, 8 July 1986, Ser A No 103, (1986) 8 EHRR 407.
[35] *Stjerna v Finland*, 25 Nov 1994, Ser A No 299-B, (1997) 24 EHRR 195.
[36] Eg *Rees v UK*, 17 Oct 1986, Ser A No 106, [1987] 2 FLR 111.
[37] Eg *Dudgeon v UK*, 22 Oct 1981, Ser A No 45, (1981) 4 EHRR 149.

and non-private spheres of daily life in cases where 'professional and non-professional activities were so intermingled that there was no means of distinguishing between them':

> 'There appears, furthermore, to be no reason of principle why this understanding of the notion of "private life" should be taken to exclude activities of a professional or business nature since it is, after all, in the course of their working lives that the majority of people have a significant, if not the greatest, opportunity of developing relationships with the outside world. . . . [I]t is not always possible to distinguish clearly which of an individual's activities form part of his professional or business life and which do not. Thus, especially in the case of a person exercising a liberal profession, his work in that context may form part and parcel of his life to such a degree that it becomes impossible to know in what capacity he is acting at a given moment of time.'[38]

The conclusion is thus that what is covered by 'respect for private life' under the Convention is much more than merely the right to be protected from publicity (the traditional meaning associated with 'privacy' in Anglo-American systems[39]). Protection from unwanted press intrusion is implicit in the concept of 'respect for private life' in situations where such publicity could indeed 'comprise to a certain degree the right to establish and develop relationships with other human beings' as the Court put it in *Niemietz*. The values underpinning this guarantee involve those of choice of lifestyle and development of an individual's personality.[40] However, individuals may voluntarily place themselves outside the scope of protection from social or moral inhibition promoted by unwanted publicity. Thus the Commission has accepted that respect for private life includes 'the right to privacy, the right to live as far as one wishes, protected from publicity',[41] but always subject to the recognition that an individual by his own actions may bring 'his private life into contact with public life or into close connection with other protected interests'.[42] This recognition is also appropriate in considering Article 10's guarantee of freedom of expression in relation to protection of the rights of politicians who by definition have brought themselves within the public domain.[43]

The formulation in which Article 8 is expressed is adopted in subsequent guarantees. As with Article 8's requirement of 'respect' for private and family life, home and correspondence, so thought, conscience and religion (Article 9), expression (Article 10), and peaceful public protest (Article 11) are given specific

---

[38] *Niemietz v Germany*, 16 Dec 1992, Ser A No 251-B, at para 29, (1993) 16 EHRR 97.
[39] Drzemczewski, *The Right to Respect for Private & Family Life*, (Strasbourg, 1993) 8.
[40] Although, paradoxically, the Strasbourg Court can restrict 'lifestyle choices' or uphold domestic laws which may inhibit such through operation of the 'margin of appreciation' in situations where there is little European consensus: cf *Sheffield and Horsham v United Kingdom*, 30 July 1998, RJD 1998-V, 2011, (no requirement on the part of a state to alter register of births to recognise post-operative transsexual identity); *Laskey, Jaggard and Brown v United Kingdom*, 19 Feb 1997, RJD 1997-I, 120 (prohibition on sado-masochistic practices upheld).
[41] Cf Application No 6825/74, *X v Iceland*, DR 5, 86.
[42] Application No 6959/75, *Brüggeman and Scheuten v Germany*, DR 10, 100 at 115.
[43] In particular, *Lingens* case, note 34 above, discussed below at p 63.

recognition in paragraph 1 of each Article. Thereafter, however, each guarantee is subject to the exceptions provided by paragraph 2 which identifies particular state interests which may justify interference with individual rights, always provided any interference is 'in accordance with the law' (or 'prescribed by law') and 'necessary in a democratic society'. This formulation thus emphasises the need to balance competing individual and community interests, but by using a more sophisticated test than that hitherto adopted in the comparatively few instances in which Scottish courts have purported to achieve this weighing of conflicting demands.[44] Greater consideration both of the question of the legitimacy of state action[45] and in particular its proportionality (a more searching requirement than that of *Wednesbury* unreasonableness) is necessary. Questions arising under these Articles are now determined using a well-established checklist: first, has there been any interference with a substantive right; second, if so, is this 'in accordance with the law'; third, does the interference purport to have a legitimate aim; and fourth, is the actual interference 'necessary in a democratic society'? Each part of the test is not without some element of difficulty.

Whether there has been any 'interference' with the guarantee is not without difficulty. The duty imposed by paragraph 1 upon states to ensure 'respect' for privacy and family life can involve both negative and positive duties: that is, there will be a duty on the state to refrain from taking action which interferes with the guarantee, and in some cases also a positive requirement to ensure that the legal system encourages or ensures effective 'respect' in the conduct of private and family life. In discussing both questions for the purposes of determination of the applicability of paragraph 1, the Court makes use of the notion of 'interference' found in the opening words of paragraph 2. Normally, the question whether a state by its action has failed to refrain from 'interfering' with an individual's rights is a straightforward one. There will be an interference when state action has a direct impact upon the individual (as, for example, with the storage and release of information concerning an individual's private life[46]). The mere existence of certain legal provisions (for example, that which renders certain forms of homosexual conduct criminal[47] or authorises telephone-tapping[48]) may also be sufficient without the necessity of establishing application of the legal powers: the 'chilling effect' (to adopt the American usage) upon an individual's behaviour may constitute in itself an 'interference'. But in addition to this essentially negative requirement to refrain from action, a state may be under a positive obligation to ensure respect. There may also be an interference through a failure by a state to take effective steps to ensure the protection of Article 8 rights, for example, by failing to provide legal safeguards, or through an inability or unwillingness to enforce such rights. Most of the development of the notion of positive duty has taken place in consideration of protection of family life rather than privacy, but further extension to privacy issues is certainly possible both by Strasbourg and in British domestic courts and by public

---

[44] Eg *Aldred* v *Miller* 1925 JC 21 (rights of assembly to be balanced with rights of other users of public parks).
[45] Cf *Malone* v *Metropolitan Police Commissioner* (No 2) [1979] Ch 344 (no law prohibiting telephone tapping by state officials, therefore prima facie lawful).
[46] *Leander* v *Sweden* 26 Mar 1987, Ser A No 116, para 48, (1987) 9 EHRR 433.
[47] Eg *Dudgeon* case, note 37 above, para 41.
[48] Eg *Klass* case, note 26 above, para 41.

authorities under the mandate of the Human Rights Act. Examples of breaches of positive duties in family law issues include unsatisfactory, generally applicable rules of private law (as with discriminatory treatment of illegitimate children[49]), failures to recognise certain legal rights (such as those which can ensure that a party to a marriage can relieve himself or herself of the duty to cohabit[50]) and outcomes which inhibit 'respect' for family life (as with a legal rule which made it impossible for a mother to deny the paternity of her husband[51]).

Any interference involving a failure to refrain from action must be 'in accordance with the law' and also have a legitimate aim. The first requirement calls for scrutiny of both the extent to which state activity is covered by domestic legal rules, and also the quality of these rules themselves. Absolute certainty and clarity are not essential: 'many laws are inevitably couched in terms which, to a greater or lesser extent, are vague and whose interpretation and application are questions of practice'[52] and as long as there is reasonable foreseeability of the consequences of any action, the requirement will be satisfied. The law itself must also conform to the notion of the rule of law—that is, there must be some safeguard against arbitrariness in its application.[53] However, Strasbourg supervision of domestic compliance with such legislation is limited: the initial responsibility for securing the correct interpretation of such law rests with national courts.[54] The test of 'legitimate aim' rarely (if ever) poses substantial problems since invariably the interference can be brought under one of the goals listed under paragraph 2—national security, public safety, national economic well-being, prevention of disorder or crime, protection of health, protection of morals, or protection of the rights of others.

The final issue in any Article 8 question gives rise to the real complexity in Strasbourg jurisprudence, that is the determination as to whether any interference is 'necessary in a democratic society'. The state's justification is subject to searching scrutiny. Resolution of any question of invasion of privacy sufficiently serious to amount to an 'interference' involves consideration of the reasons advanced, and the application of a test of proportionality: whether the relationship between the action taken and the aim of the intervention is acceptable. This may involve the Strasbourg Court in considering whether the domestic law or practice in question is out of line with standards generally applied elsewhere in Europe, for it will be easier to condemn state interference as not being 'necessary in a democratic society' if the great majority of other European states follow a different policy (as, for example, in having decriminalised homosexual behaviour[55]). However, at Strasbourg level, the recognition of a 'margin of appreciation' confers a certain amount of discretion on state authorities in determining the outcome of any test of proportionality.[56] This is a

---

[49] *Marckx v Belgium*, 13 June 1979, Ser A No 31, para 31, (1979) 2 EHRR 330.
[50] *Airey v Ireland*, 9 Oct 1979, Ser A No 32, para 32, (1979–80) 2 EHRR 305; cf *Johnston v Ireland*, 18 Dec 1986, Ser A No 112 (Convention to be read as a whole; and thus no positive duty to ensure the availability of divorce since Art 12 excludes such).
[51] *Kroon v Netherlands*, 27 Oct 1994, Ser A No 297-C, (1995) 19 EHRR 263.
[52] *Sunday Times v UK*, 26 Apr 1979, Ser A No 30, at para 47, (1979–80) 2 EHRR 245.
[53] *Malone v UK*, 2 Aug 1984, Ser A No 82, at paras 67–68, (1984) 7 EHRR 14.
[54] *Chappell v UK*, 30 Mar 1989, Ser A No 152-A.
[55] *Dudgeon* case, note 37 above, at para 60.
[56] For recent discussion, see Ovey, 'The Margin of Appreciation and Article 8' (1998) 19 HRLJ 10.

recognition on the part of the Court that national decision-makers are better placed than European institutions in determining the outcome of any process involving the balancing of individual and collective interests on account of 'their direct and continuous contact with the vital forces of their countries'.[57] It is an affirmation of the Court's status as an international tribunal rather than a final court of appeal for domestic matters, and of the emphasis placed by the European Convention on Human Rights on the primary role of national authorities in ensuring the effective securing of Convention guarantees. Yet it is not a negation of the Court's supervisory task, for it has been at pains to emphasise the retention of a power of review of any assessment at domestic level.[58] The extent of any 'margin of appreciation', too, will depend upon both the aim of the restriction and also the nature of the activities involved: where a case involves 'a most intimate aspect of private life', the extent of state discretion in determining the proportionality of the interference will be limited,[59] but much wider discretion is appropriate when economic or fiscal policy matters are in question.[60]

Could Britain's lack of a law of privacy be seen to be a breach of its obligations? If so, could domestic courts and 'public authorities' begin to construct a set of guarantees under the authority of the Human Rights Act and Article 8? An over-intrusive press may not be a peculiarly British phenomenon, but when placed alongside the British public's apparently insatiable appetite for gossip and the British expectation that the private lives of Ministers be beyond reproach, the lack of a domestic law of privacy preventing publication of details on private lives—many concerning the establishment and development of 'relationships with other human beings'—is perhaps felt most acutely. In determining whether a state is required to take positive steps to ensure regard for private and family life, 'regard must be had to the fair balance that has to be struck between the general interests of the community and the interests of the individual'.[61] No straightforward guidance is available from Strasbourg, but creativity at domestic level on the part of judges and the Press Complaints Commission is certainly possible, if not inevitable. One leading commentator suggests, for example, that publication of a photograph of 'that which anyone could have seen in public' is unlikely to result in a privacy interference.[62] Again, the conclusion to be drawn from the current state of Strasbourg jurisprudence is that such a development in domestic law will not be precluded, but neither is it strictly required provided always that existing devices (such as the Press Complaints Commission, or the law on breach of confidence) will be sufficiently flexible to accommodate demands for respect for privacy. A recent Commission decision illustrates this. In *Stewart-Brady* v *United Kingdom*, the applicant (a prisoner who had been convicted of the murders of three children) complained that his privacy had been breached when a book was

---

[57] *Handyside* v *United Kingdom*, 7 Dec 1976, Ser A No 24, at para 48, (1976) 1 EHRR 737.
[58] Eg *Klass* case, note 26 above, para 49.
[59] *Dudgeon* case, note 37 above, at para 52.
[60] Eg *Lithgow* v *UK*, Ser A No 102, at para 122.
[61] *Rees* case, note 36 above, para 37.
[62] Naismith, note 28 above, at 153. However, at 156 the author cites the Commission decision in Application no 20683/92, *N* v *Portugal* (unreported) in which the conviction of a magazine publisher for defamation and invasion of privacy involving the publication of photographs of a businessman involved in sexual activities with a number of women was accepted as proportionate for protection of the rights of individuals for the purposes of Art 10.

published by an author claiming to be the applicant's daughter; a further application related to a story published in a newspaper purporting to describe a sexual encounter between the author and the applicant during a prison visit. The Commission accepted that English law protected privacy through the civil law of defamation, even although the legal system did not recognise 'any actionable right of privacy as such'.[63] However, in making this point, the Commission seemed to add an element of uncertainty as to the extent to which there should be effective access to enforcement machinery through the provision of legal aid to individuals to vindicate Article 8 rights. As far as respect for family life is concerned, the Court has indicated that legal aid may require to be provided to ensure the 'effective accessibility' through the courts of a remedy of judicial separation.[64] However, here the Commission considered that a state need not provide legal aid to allow actions of defamation for harm to reputation, since this is not as vital an interest. In this respect, certain privacy values seem secondary to other Article 8 interests.

COUNTERVAILING INTERESTS IN FREE SPEECH

Privacy issues involving unwanted media intrusion cannot be considered in isolation from other Convention guarantees. In this respect, the Human Rights Act reminds judges of the danger if creativity in fashioning a protection for privacy exceeds caution in preventing harm to free speech. Courts must have particular regard to the importance of this latter interest, not only on account of section 12 of the Act, but more particularly under Article 10 of the Convention which seeks to protect freedom of expression, a guarantee which is to include the freedom 'to receive and impart information and ideas without interference by public authority'. As with Article 8, so too Article 10 itself requires the balancing of competing claims. Here, interests in speech can conflict with interests in protecting national security, public morality and, of particular importance in discussion of privacy, protection of 'the reputation or rights of others'. Again, interferences are always subject to the 'necessary in a democratic society' provision which calls for proportionality between means and ends.

For domestic courts, there is, however, potentially more guidance available from Article 10 jurisprudence for shaping domestic law to accord with Convention guarantees. The starting-point is a presumption in favour of speech, but as a tool for the enhancement of democracy and for individual personal development. The *leitmotiven* of 'pluralism, tolerance and broadmindedness without which there is no "democratic society"' are again stressed.[65] This allows for an approach to free speech which involves differing levels of protection depending upon the issue at stake. Political expression thus requires the highest safeguards, while there will be a wide margin of appreciation recognised on the part of state authorities in cases involving less worthy expression such as obscene material[66] or satirical attacks upon religious belief.[67] In *Lingens*, the applicant had published

---

[63] Application nos 27436/95 and 28406/95, 2 July 1997 (unreported).
[64] *Airey* case, note 50 above, para 33.
[65] *Handyside* case, note 57 above, at para 49.
[66] Eg *Handyside*, above; *Müller* v *Switzerland*, 24 May 1988, Ser A No 133, at para 27.
[67] *Otto-Preminger Institute* v *Austria*, 20 Sept 1994, Ser A No 295-A, (1995) 19 EHRR 34.

articles criticising the head of state's fitness for office. This had resulted in successful private defamation actions against the journalist, sanctions which were subsequently criticised by the European Court as a form of censure likely to inhibit political discussion and debate and thus 'liable to hamper the press in performing its task as purveyor of information and public watchdog'. Further, 'the limits of acceptable criticism are . . . wider as regards a politician as such than as regards a private individual' since a politician 'inevitably and knowingly lays himself open to close scrutiny of his every word and deed'. Accordingly, while protection of reputation is a recognised ground for state interference and will extend to protection of the reputation of politicians, 'in such cases the requirements of such protection have to be weighed in relation to the interests of open discussion of issues'.[68] This sentiment shapes Article 10 application. 'Freedom of the press affords the public one of the best means of discovering and forming an opinion on the ideas and attitudes of their political leaders'. Further, it aids democratic communication between the electorate and those chosen as its representatives; 'it gives politicians the opportunity to reflect and comment on the preoccupations of public opinion; it thus enables everyone to participate in the free political debate which is at the very core of the concept of a political society'.[69] Yet there are limits. In *Prager and Oberschlick* v *Austria*, harsh criticisms of a judge's personal integrity fell outwith Article 10 protection since these had not been made in good faith and had violated principles of professional ethics.[70] In other words, the media should be able to discharge their function of contributing to political debate and accountability without exceeding generally acceptable standards.

CONCLUSION

What principles can be extracted, then, from Article 8 and 10 case-law to help shape any new law of privacy which also respects the importance of freedom of expression? There is no ready-made package available for instant use, largely since the Strasbourg organs have been keen to stress the primary responsibility of national decision-makers to ensure Convention guarantees are met. However, three principles emerge. First, there is a hierarchy of protected rights or interests, with democracy a fundamental value to be accorded the highest safeguards. Second, other fundamental values such as tolerance and broadmindedness are of importance in applying the test of whether any interference is 'necessary in a democratic society', a phrase which suggests some 'pressing social need' rather than the wider latitude implied by more flexible expressions such as 'useful', 'reasonable', or 'desirable'.[71] Any reasons advanced for any interference must be both 'relevant' and 'sufficient'.[72] Third, 'private life' cannot be restrained by any notion of 'inner circle', and must extend to 'the right to develop relationship with other human beings', including in certain cases professional relationships.[73]

These three principles in particular provide new starting-points for the resol-

---

[68] *Lingens* case, note 34 above, at paras 42–44.
[69] *Castells* v *Spain*, 23 Apr 1992, Ser A No 236, at para 43 (sub nom *Castes* v *Spain*) (1992) 14 EHRR 445.
[70] 26 April 1995, Ser A No 313, (1996) 21 EHRR 1.
[71] *Dudgeon* case, note 37 above, at paras 51 and 53.
[72] Eg *Olsson* v *Sweden* (No 2), 27 Nov 1992, Ser A No 250, paras 87–91, (1994) 17 EHRR 134.
[73] *Niemietz* case, note 38 above, at para 29.

ution of recurring problems in media self-regulation, and should help resolve disposals by the Press Complaints Commission of complaints and by the courts of litigation seeking to rely upon Article 8's requirement of 'respect for private life'. Invasions into the privacy of political figures—individuals who have 'knowingly [lain themselves] open to close scrutiny of . . . every word and deed'—are more likely to be able to be justified if such invasions contribute meaningfully to political accountability. Yet there are limits. The values implicit in pluralism and respect for private life cannot support the stigmatisation of certain forms of private conduct such as homosexual practices even if others find such behaviour immoral or are 'shocked, offended or disturbed' by it.[74] Protection of a politician's private lifestyle and choice of social contacts will require more weighty consideration before exposure. These principles should certainly provide clearer guidance on whether publication of information on a range of standard media stories can continue to be justified: whether exposure of the sexual orientation of a Government Minister or an MP, or the sex lives of television soap-actors or heirs to the throne can continue to be effectively ignored by the Press Complaints Commission. Yet the European Convention on Human Rights is no charter against publication of details of hypocrisy or corruption: to the contrary, the watchdog role of the media is recognised and acknowledged where there is a story of double standards or cronyism. The Cabinet Minister who publicly asserts his belief in family values while surreptitiously entertaining a mistress should rightly fail in any attempt to attack the press for invading his privacy, although any 'outing' of another Minister as homosexual for no purpose other than to disclose this fact to the public should rightly be condemned as unjustified and failing Convention tests of interest or proportionality. The conclusion must be that incorporation of the Convention will bring with it a healthier respect for tolerance, plurality of opinion and broadmindedness which will in practical terms also result in a more explicit regard for privacy. The increased regard for these values and concern for individual rights as a whole will prove to be a perfect complement to the enhanced democracy that devolution should bring to Scotland.

---

[74] Cf *Dudgeon* case, note 37 above, at para 60.

5: OPENING UP GOVERNMENT: PARADISE POSTPONED—AGAIN?[1]

Mark Poustie

INTRODUCTION: THE IMPORTANCE OF FREEDOM OF INFORMATION

The value of freedom of information ('FOI') in making government more open and accountable and in promoting better informed discussion of public affairs should be readily apparent.[2] On a more personal level FOI may be of considerable assistance to individuals who wish to check what information about them is held by public and private bodies to ensure that it is accurate and to prevent abuse of the information. Indeed the United Nations General Assembly has stated: 'Freedom of information is a fundamental human right and is the touchstone for all the freedoms to which the United Nations is consecrated.'[3]

However, FOI certainly should not be seen as some kind of panacea for society's ills. It is but one aspect of a more general move towards more participative and transparent forms of governance.

Moreover, no one would argue that FOI should be absolute. There are areas of government activity, for example those involving national security, in relation to which there is a legitimate interest in keeping information confidential and about which no one would expect to be able to obtain information. In addition while personal information such as medical records ought to be available to the subject of the information, few would argue that it ought to be available to third parties.

The balance between opening up government under an FOI regime and the need to preserve confidentiality and privacy in some cases is a key issue in the FOI debate. The balance is explicitly addressed in the application of the grounds for refusing access to information in existing and proposed FOI legislation.

It must also be remembered that an FOI regime will apply to public authorities and some private bodies performing public functions. It will not cover information held and processed by private bodies not performing public functions, for example a supermarket studying the spending habits of loyalty card holders.[4] This raises another key issue in FOI: the relationship between the data protection regime which seeks to protect privacy by preventing abuse of personal data and

---

[1] For an excellent and detailed treatment of the subject (excluding the Labour administration's 1997 White Paper), see Birkinshaw, *Freedom of Information* (2nd edn, Butterworths, 1996). For a more concise review (again excluding the Labour administration's 1997 White Paper) see Finch and Ashton, *Administrative Law in Scotland* (W Green/Sweet & Maxwell, 1997), ch 6.
[2] Indeed these are some of the key aims in Lord Lucas' Freedom of Information Bill, which is before Parliament at the time of writing, together with enabling more effective public participation in law and policy-making and administration (cl 1(1)).
[3] UN General Assembly Resolution 59(2), 14 December 1946.
[4] Although such actions would be subject to the Data Protection Act 1998 which would enable individuals to obtain access to such information and have it rectified if it is inaccurate. See further below at pp 74–75.

any proposed FOI regime which will be designed to promote openness. Much information on the activities of the private sector is nonetheless open to varying degrees of public scrutiny.[5]

This chapter briefly outlines the historical development of FOI legislation, the extent to which the European Convention on Human Rights ('ECHR') and the Human Rights Act 1998 provide a right of access to information and the problematic relationship between FOI and national security. It then proceeds to review existing FOI provisions including those relating to personal information such as the data protection regime. Thereafter it discusses UK-wide and Scottish developments under the present administration and access to information at European Union level.

DEVELOPMENT OF FOI LEGISLATION

The traditional secrecy of and control of information by Government institutions in the United Kingdom is well known and documented elsewhere.[6] Despite its adherence to excessive secrecy and in spite of embarrassing attempts to control information such as the Spycatcher litigation,[7] the previous Conservative administration nevertheless introduced a range of statutory and non-statutory FOI measures. These included specific statutory rights to local government information generally,[8] environmental information,[9] and personal information.[10] A relatively comprehensive but non-statutory 'Code of Practice on Access to Government Information' (the 'UK Code of Practice') was also introduced in 1994[11] following the 1993 White Paper 'Open Government'.[12] Many of these developments stemmed from the Conservative administrations' ideological commitment to market forces whereby citizens could not be effective players in the market or consumers of public services without access to adequate information.[13] The perceived shortcomings of local government, including concerns about corruption, were also a significant driving force behind the measures relating to local government.[14] Fears relating to abuse of personal data—so much easier in the information technology age—were also apparent.[15] Much credit for these developments should also go to bodies such as the Campaign for Freedom of Information ('CFOI') which have worked tirelessly for a comprehensive FOI

[5] Basic information on companies is available from Companies House under the Companies Act 1985 while information, for example, on applications to operate polluting processes or dispose of waste is available on public registers under eg the Environmental Protection Act 1990, ss 20 and 64.
[6] Birkinshaw, op cit, note 1 above, chs 3 & 4. See also Ponting, *Secrecy in Britain* (1990).
[7] See eg *Attorney General v Guardian Newspapers Ltd (No 2)* [1990] 1 AC 109; and Birkinshaw, op cit, note 1 above, ch 3.
[8] For example, by means of the Local Government (Access to Information) Act 1985 which amended the Local Government (Scotland) Act 1973 (see also below at pp 73).
[9] For example, under the Environmental Protection Act 1990, ss 20, 64 and 120 and the Environmental Information Regulations 1992 (SI 1992/3240). See further below at pp 76–82.
[10] See eg Access to Personal Files Act 1987; and Access to Medical Records Act 1988.
[11] See now 'Code of Practice on Access to Government Information' (2nd edn, 1997) and 'Code of Practice on Access to Scottish Executive Information' (July 1999).
[12] Cm 2290, July 1993.
[13] See eg 'This Common Inheritance: Britain's Environmental Strategy', Cm 1200, 1990, para 1.20.
[14] See eg Birkinshaw, op cit, note 1 above, pp 134ff.
[15] See eg the Data Protection Act 1984 and now the Data Protection Act 1998.

regime.[16] European and international requirements also lay behind some of these developments.[17] However, while FOI regimes have developed apace elsewhere,[18] the United Kingdom has developed no more than a fragmented and uncoordinated patchwork of provisions and the past twenty years are littered with the detritus of failed FOI legislation.[19]

Although the Conservative administration sought to make local government more accountable, it resisted claims that central government too should be made more accountable despite the fact that the same arguments to justify more accountability could be applied at national level and perhaps even more persuasively. For example, central government misuse of information has included covering up the facts of the sinking of the Argentinian warship, the *General Belgrano*,[20] misleading Parliament about arms exports to Iraq and allowing the prosecution of parties in the Matrix Churchill affair which involved arms exports to Iraq.[21] The record of the central government-controlled nuclear industry in the United Kingdom for being open and accountable would be laughable were it not so appalling.[22]

The introduction of the 'UK Code of Practice' could be viewed as a concession that the arguments which the Conservative government had employed to open up local government to public scrutiny applied with equal force to itself. However, a non-binding 'UK Code of Practice', enforceable on the recommendation of an Ombudsman alone, is no substitute for a legally enforceable statutory right. Indeed, if statutory rights were acceptable for certain areas of central government activity, such as environmental protection, why not for all government activity?

The current Labour administration, which had included a commitment to an FOI Act in its election manifesto, published a White Paper, 'Your Right to Know—The Government's proposals for a Freedom of Information Act' ('Your Right to Know') in December 1997.[23] Legislation was promised in 1998–99. However, FOI legislation was not included in the 1998–99 legislative programme. A draft UK Bill finally emerged in May 1999 together with a consultation paper, 'Freedom of Information: Consultation on Draft Legislation' ('Consultation on Draft Legislation').[24] Subsequently the Scottish Executive adopted its own 'Code of

---

[16] The CFOI was largely responsible for promoting the Local Government (Access to Information) Act 1985.
[17] Eg the Directive 90/313 on freedom of access to information on the environment is implemented by the Environmental Information Regulations 1992 (SI 1992/3240).
[18] Sweden (established in 18th century), USA (since 1966), France (since 1978), Canada, Australia and New Zealand (since 1982) and the Netherlands (since 1991): 'Your Right to Know—The Government's proposals for a Freedom of Information Act', Cm 3818, 1997, para 1.3.
[19] Eg between 1977 and 1979 four FOI Bills were introduced. In 1992 CFOI and Mark Fisher MP introduced a Right to Know Bill. Most recently Lord Lucas introduced an FOI Bill in the Lords in anticipation of the UK Government's FOI Bill.
[20] The disclosure of this information to Tam Dalyell MP by Clive Ponting, a senior civil servant in the Ministry of Defence, led to Ponting's prosecution under s 2 of the Official Secrets Act 1911 and subsequent acquittal: *R v Ponting* [1985] Crim LR 318. This acquittal was partially responsible for the repeal of s 2 and its replacement by the Official Secrets Act 1989. See further below at pp 71–73.
[21] This led to the Scott inquiry 'Inquiry into the Export of Defence Equipment and Dual-Use Goods to Iraq and Related Prosecutions and its report', Rt Hon Sir Richard Scott, V-C (commonly known as the Scott Report), published on 16 February 1996: 1995–96, HC 115. See also Tomkins, 'Government Information and Parliament: Misleading by Design or by Default?' [1996] PL 472.
[22] See eg Poustie & Demick, 'Developments at Dounreay' [1998] 10 ELM 231.
[23] Cm 3818, 1997.
[24] Cm 4355, May 1999. UK Legislation was subsequently introduced in Parliament, although it has not completed its passage at the time of writing.

Practice' (the 'Scottish Code of Practice') in relation to information held by Scottish public bodies within the jurisdiction of the Scottish Parliamentary Commissioner for Administration.[25] The Deputy First Minister has also announced that the Scottish Executive will be enacting its own FOI legislation in relation to information held by such bodies as early as possible and that the 'Scottish Code of Practice' will only remain in force until that legislation is enacted.[26] A consultation paper has since followed.[27]

Finally, progress at European Union level towards an FOI regime for the institutions of the European Union has been very limited.[28]

IMPACT OF THE ECHR AND THE HUMAN RIGHTS ACT 1998

It might be thought that the enactment of an FOI Act is actually unnecessary given the enactment of the Human Rights Act 1998 which incorporates much of the ECHR into domestic law. Will this not provide a kind of backdoor FOI Act? Unfortunately, the answer is no. This might seem strange given that the language of Article 10 of the ECHR appears to extend to access to information.[29] However, the jurisprudence of the Strasbourg authorities clearly indicates that Article 10 does not provide a general right of access to information. The general duty on the state appears to be not to obstruct access to information which is available rather than to make information available.[30] The European Court of Human Rights has also held that the right to receive and impart information includes the right to seek out information, but only to the extent that it is already available.[31]

A right of access to information may also be found in Article 8 in certain circumstances. In *Gaskin* v *United Kingdom*[32] the applicant sought information held by a public authority in relation to the period he had spent in foster care. The denial of access to this information was held to be a breach of Article 8(1). The majority of the Court gave considerable weight to what the information meant to the applicant rather than to any use he might have wished to make of it. The Court, however, explicitly noted that it was expressing no opinion on whether a general right of access to data and information could be derived from Article 8(1). In *Guerra* v *Italy*[33] although the failure of the Italian authorities to provide members of the public with an emergency plan for dealing with a major accident at a chemical plant as required by Italian and EC law did not amount to a breach of Article 10, it did breach Article 8 as severe environmental pollution could affect

---

[25] 'Code of Practice on Access to Scottish Executive Information', July 1999. Schedule 1 lists the bodies to which it applies.
[26] Scottish Office News Releases 1076/99, 24 May 1999 and 1311/99, 23 June 1999.
[27] Scottish Executive, 'An Open Scotland - Freedom of Information: a Consultation', November 1999 ('An Open Scotland').
[28] See further below at pp 95–97.
[29] Art 10(1): 'Everyone has the right to freedom of expression. This right shall include freedom to hold opinions and *to receive and impart information* and ideas without interference by public authority and regardless of frontiers . . . .' (emphasis added).
[30] See *Leander* v *Sweden* (1987) 9 EHRR 433; *Z* v *Austria* No. 10392/83 56 DR 13 (1988). See also *Guerra* v *Italy* (1998) 26 EHRR 357.
[31] *Z* v *Austria*, note 29 above.
[32] (1990) 12 EHRR 36.
[33] (1998) 26 EHRR 357.

the wellbeing of members of the public and prevent them from enjoying their private and family lives.

A SPECIAL CASE: FOI AND NATIONAL SECURITY ISSUES[34]

National security and freedom of information are not happy bedfellows. National security 'poses the most difficult of questions about executive action and its relationship with effective accountability and informed public opinion'.[35] It raises questions about what we know or ought to know about the security and intelligence services and about the ways in which they gather and make use of information. The reputation of the services was damaged considerably under the last government with revelations about penetration by the KGB and allegations about dirty tricks.

However, since then there has been considerable progress, mostly as a result of actual or anticipated proceedings before the European Court of Human Rights.[36] The three security and intelligence services, the Security Service (MI5), the Secret Intelligence Service (MI6/SIS) and the Government Communications Headquarters (GCHQ) are now on a statutory footing to deflect claims about the lack of legal foundation for secret surveillance.[37] Their functions are now at least partially defined, albeit very widely.[38] With the extension of the Security Service's role into work in support of the police, there are strong arguments that it should be more publicly accountable. Each service has a Commissioner who oversees the role of the Secretary of State or the Scottish Ministers as appropriate in relation to granting warrants for interception of communications or interference with property and wireless telegraphy.[39] One of the Commissioners' functions is to report annually to the Prime Minister on the supervision of each service. The Prime Minister must lay the report before Parliament subject to editing out any matters prejudicial to national security or the functioning of the services. None of the Commissioners has yet found any significant problem in the operation of the Acts. Tribunals have been established for investigating complaints in relation to telephone tapping and the other functions of the services.[40] Although, remarkably, no complaint has yet been successful before any of the three tribunals and the right of appeal to the courts is excluded in all cases, the tribunals probably satisfy the requirements of the ECHR as regards provision of an effective

---

[34] See generally Lustgarten & Leigh, *In From the Cold—National Security and Parliamentary Democracy*, (Clarendon Press, 1994).
[35] Birkinshaw, op cit, note 1 above, p 26.
[36] *Malone v United Kingdom* (1984) 7 EHRR 14 led to the introduction of statutory controls in the Interception of Communications Act 1985 over telephone tapping by the police and Security Service and the Commission's decision in *Hewitt and Harman v United Kingdom* (1992) 14 EHRR 657, indicated the need to put the security and intelligence services on a statutory footing—see note 36 below.
[37] See the Security Service Act 1989 in relation to the Security Service; and the Intelligence Services Act 1994 in relation to SIS and GCHQ.
[38] Security Service: Security Service Act 1989 (as amended by the Security Service Act 1996), s 1(2)–(4); Secret Intelligence Service: Intelligence Services Act 1994, s 1; GCHQ: ibid, s 3.
[39] Interception of Communications Act 1985, s 8; Security Service Act 1989, s 4; Intelligence Services Act 1994, s 8.
[40] Interception of Communications Act 1985, s 7; Security Service Act 1989, s 5; and Intelligence Services Act 1994, s 9.

remedy.[41] A joint Parliamentary Committee, known as the Intelligence and Security Committee, has been established to examine the expenditure, administration and policy of the three services.[42] 'Like the Commissioners, it reports annually to the Prime Minister who must, again, lay the report before Parliament after editing out any material prejudicial to the services. Although these provisions are not as comprehensive as some,[43] they are a great advance on the previous non-statutory regime. Both the Security Service and GCHQ have also developed informative websites.[44] Given that 20 years ago, Government was still denying that these services even existed, these advances are remarkable.

However, at the same time, disclosure of information relating to national security in the public interest has been made much harder. This is largely the result of *R v Ponting* and the *Spycatcher* litigation (see below) which showed up deficiencies (from a Government perspective) both in the protection of official information under the Official Secrets Act 1911 and, where the Act did not apply, under the law of confidentiality.

The much-criticised section 2 of the Official Secrets Act 1911 made it an offence for a person holding office under Her Majesty to communicate official information to any person other than a person to whom he was authorised to communicate it, or a person to whom it was his duty in the interest of the state to communicate it. In *R v Ponting*,[45] the defendant argued that it was in the interest of the state for him to communicate information regarding the sinking of the Argentinian warship, the *General Belgrano*, to Tam Dalyell MP as the information revealed that the Government was deliberately misleading the House of Commons and a Select Committee about the sinking. The judge directed the jury that the interests of state were synonymous with the interests of the Government of the day. He also ruled that 'duty' in the section meant official duty, not moral or public duty. Despite his clear direction to convict Ponting, the jury acquitted him.

In addition, in the *Spycatcher* litigation the Government found that it was ultimately unable to rely on the law of confidentiality to prevent publication of the ex-MI5 officer Peter Wright's allegations of dirty tricks by his former employers.[46] This was largely because the matter was already in the public domain, having been published in Australia and the United States, and it was pointless to try to prevent further publication.

These two developments led to the Official Secrets Act 1989. In relation to both security, intelligence and defence information and international relations any disclosure which is damaging is an offence.[47] In addition, the disclosure of any information on law enforcement is an offence regardless of whether or not it is damaging. There is no public interest defence as there was in section 2 of the 1911 Act. Any officer who works for the security and intelligence services is thus under a lifetime duty of confidentiality unless of course the Government waives

---

[41] See *Christie v United Kingdom* (1994) 78-A DR 119.
[42] Intelligence Services Act 1994, s 10.
[43] See, for example, the German system discussed in *Klass v Germany* (1978) 2 EHRR 214.
[44] http://www.mi5.gov.uk/ and http://www.gchq.gov.uk/.
[45] [1985] Crim LR 318.
[46] *Attorney General v Guardian Newspapers Ltd (No 2)* [1990] 1 AC 109. See also *Lord Advocate v Scotsman Publications Ltd* 1989 SLT 705, [1989] 1 AC 812.
[47] Official Secrets Act 1989, s 1.

confidentiality.[48] However, no offence is committed by a third party who comes into possession of information obtained without authority unless the third party makes a further disclosure and has reasonable cause to believe that the disclosure would be damaging.

CURRENT PROVISIONS ON FOI

Access to local government information

As mentioned above the Conservative administrations subjected local government to a rigorous freedom of information regime. The Local Government (Scotland) Act 1973 requires each authority to keep open for inspection at all reasonable hours a book of pecuniary interests, for example in contracts that members have (sections 38–49). The Local Government (Access to Information) Act 1985 amended the Local Government (Scotland) Act 1973, inserting provisions requiring access to council meetings and to the agendas and papers for such meetings (sections 50A–B). Minutes of meetings and background papers may also be inspected (sections 50C–D). All these provisions are extended to committee and subcommittee meetings (section 50E). There is a range of exceptions, including information on tenants and employees, instructions to and opinions of counsel (section 50J and Schedule 7A). Information requested must be provided at least three clear working days prior to the meeting.[49] Interestingly, however, in the context of planning the English High Court has held that there may be a duty to supply the information earlier to enable the requester to make an effective representation.[50] There are also rights to environmental information held by local authorities and these are considered further below.

The Local Government (Scotland) Act 1973 also provides that at each audit of a local authority's accounts, 'any persons interested' may inspect and make copies of the accounts and all background information (section 101(1)). The Court of Session has held that a council tax payer in a council's area falls within the definition of 'any persons interested', that motive for inspection of the background information is irrelevant and that for the period the accounts are available for inspection, the council must make arrangements to provide access to the background documentation to such persons 'however irksome to the officials it may be'.[51]

Access to personal information

In other countries, access to personal information has been one of the most widely

---

[48] This has been done on a number of occasions, eg in relation to works by former members of the Government Code and Cipher School (the forerunner of GCHQ) regarding its operations during the Second World War. See eg Hinsley & Stripp (eds), *Code Breakers—The Inside Story of Bletchley Park* (OUP, 1993); Smith, *Station X, The Codebreakers of Bletchley Park* (Channel 4 Books, 1998).
[49] This is the overall effect of the Local Government (Scotland) Act 1973, ss 50B(1), (3) and 50H(2)(b).
[50] R v *Rochdale Metropolitan Borough Council, ex p Brown* [1997] Env LR 100, QBD.
[51] *Stirrat v City of Edinburgh Council* 1998 SCLR 971, [1998] 10 ELM 220.

used aspects of FOI legislation.[52] The regime is largely based upon the Data Protection Act 1998 which has replaced the Data Protection Act 1984 and the Access to Personal Files Act 1987 although there are other provisions discussed below which still provide access to specific types of information.

Data Protection Act 1998[53]

The principal legislation in this area is now the Data Protection Act 1998.[54] Its purpose is to subject data processing to certain safeguards known as the data protection principles (Schedule 1, Part I) to prevent abuse and to ensure that individuals ('data subjects', section 1(1)) who are the subjects of personal data held for processing by data controllers (section 1(1))[55] have a right of access to that data and a right to prevent processing in certain cases and are able to rectify or erase mistakes and obtain compensation where appropriate (Part II). One of the major changes in the law is that the 1998 Act has extended the data protection regime to 'relevant filing systems' ie manual filing systems which are structured in such a way that information on an individual is readily accessible (section 1(1)). The Access to Personal Files Act 1987 previously provided individuals with the right to see the manual files that local authorities held on them relating to social services and housing tenancies which were not covered by the Data Protection Act 1984.[56] Access to the courts was possible if a file was inaccurate. The 1987 Act has now been repealed and access to such information is now via the Data Protection Act 1998. There are various exemptions in Part IV where data need not be disclosed by the data controller. These include national security, crime and taxation. The Secretary of State or the Scottish Ministers as appropriate may also by order exempt data from disclosure, for example, in relation to the mental or physical health of the data subject.

A key feature of the 1984 Act regime was the Data Protection Registrar. His functions were to create a register of data users (now known as 'data controllers') as registration was a prerequisite of being allowed to process data, and to ensure that data users complied with the legislation including complying with the data protection principles. If an application for registration was rejected, a right of appeal existed to the Data Protection Tribunal. Appeals against enforcement measures taken by the Registrar also went to the Tribunal. Whenever data were to be processed the user carrying out the processing had to be registered. The Registrar's functions continue much as before under the 1998 Act although the name of the Registrar is now the Data Protection Commissioner (section 6, Part V and sections 51–54). It is still an offence to process data without the data controller being registered (sections 17 and 21).

---

[52] 'Your Right to Know', para 4.1.
[53] On which see generally Lloyd, *A Guide to the Data Protection Act 1998* (Butterworths, 1998). The Act was not yet fully in force at the time of writing.
[54] The Act implements Directive 95/46/EC on the protection of individuals with regard to the processing of personal data and on the free movement of such data (OJ L281, 24.10.95).
[55] Formerly known as data users under the 1984 Act.
[56] Access to Personal Files Act 1987, s 1. The Access to Personal Files (Social Work) (Scotland) Regulations 1989 (SI 1989/251); Access to Personal Files (Housing) (Scotland) Regulations 1992 (SI 1992/1852) made under the 1987 Act make more detailed provision.

There is obvious potential for overlap and conflict between an FOI Act and the Data Protection Act 1998. As regards conflict, the aims of the two regimes are at odds: the FOI Act is designed to ensure openness and accessibility whereas the 1998 Act is intended to ensure privacy.

In relation to this overlap, 'Your Right to Know' proposed that the FOI Act should not be restricted to particular types of files and so in that sense it should have a wider scope than the 1998 Act. However, the FOI Act will obviously only apply to public authorities (although that term may certainly encompass some private sector bodies such as utilities) whereas the Data Protection Act 1998 extends over all data controllers in the public and private sectors. 'Your Right to Know' proposed that the FOI Act would also enable individuals to gain access to information about themselves in addition to the data protection regime and that all rights applying under the 1998 Act should apply under the FOI Act in relation to information held on individuals by public authorities. However, in relation to access to information about oneself the UK FOI Bill provides that access should take place through the provisions of the Data Protection Act 1998.[57] This is done by making amendments to that Act and by providing that any information to which a request for information relates is exempt information if it constitutes personal data of which the applicant is the data subject. Where personal information is sought about third parties, if disclosure does not contravene the data protection principles in the 1998 Act, there will be a right to it under the FOI legislation. Under the Data Protection Act 1998, a person has the right to prevent processing in certain cases and may rectify or erase mistakes and obtain compensation where appropriate. One can foresee that considerable public education will be required to ensure that applicants make their request for information under the correct statute. However, in order to integrate the two regimes more effectively, the Data Protection Commissioner becomes the UK Information Commissioner (see also pp 93–95 below). This should enable an appropriate balance between privacy and freedom of information to be struck. Although the attempts at integration between the two regimes are positive there is still room for confusion and this makes it all the more disappointing that the two pieces of legislation were not considered by Parliament together.[58] In Scotland, the position will unfortunately be more complex, as the Scottish Information Commissioner, who will administer the Scottish FOI regime, will not be a Scottish Data Protection Registar. This will, as 'An Open Scottish' evisages, require effective liaison with the UK information Commissioner/Data Protection Registrar.

Other provisions

A range of other measures exists enabling individuals to obtain access to information held on them. For example, the Access to Health Records Act 1990 provides access to information relating to the physical or mental health of an individual by a health professional subject to certain possible exemptions.[59] Explanations must

---

[57] 'Freedom of Information: Consultation on Draft Legislation', Cm 4355, May 1999, para 32. This approach is maintained in the UK FOI Bill.
[58] See eg Lloyd, *A Guide to the Data Protection Act 1998*, p 9.
[59] Other provisions include the Access to Medical Reports Act 1988; School Pupils Records (Scotland) Regulations 1990 and the Human Fertilisation and Embryology Act 1990.

be provided where the information is not intelligible and fees may be charged in certain circumstances. Subjects have the right to correct the information. Applications to enforce duties must be made to the courts. The development of a comprehensive FOI regime raises the question of the future of this legislation. For the sake of an integrated and co-ordinated approach, it might be better to repeal and replace these various specific regimes by a general regime in an FOI Act.

Access to planning and environmental information[60]

Introduction

One area where very considerable progress has been made in increasing transparency has been in the area of access to planning and environmental information. It is instructive to consider this area as considerable research has been conducted into the effectiveness of the legislation.[61] This section focuses on two mechanisms designed to provide access to such information: public registers and the Environmental Information Regulations 1992.[62]

It was not ever thus. In the past such information was not normally made available to the public. Indeed disclosure of such information without the consent of the person supplying it was often criminalised.[63] Government thought it knew best and that there was no need to inform the public, while business was worried, firstly, that information would be misinterpreted by activists and would result in vexatious litigation damaging to industry, secondly, that confidential information would become available to competitors and, lastly, that the costs of providing information would be excessive. As late as 1984 the CBI described the system of water pollution registers introduced by the Control of Pollution Act 1974 as 'a busybody's charter'.[64] However, in recent years a complete policy reversal has resulted in a considerable amount of environmental information becoming publicly available.

This change of policy has resulted from a variety of factors. Domestically these included ongoing pressure from the Royal Commission on Environmental Pollution from 1974 onwards and the White Paper 'This Common Inheritance: Britain's Environmental Strategy' (Cm 1200, 1990) which argued that giving people information puts them in a better position to make their own consumer decisions, to exert pressure for change and was the best way of stimulating public discussion and earning public confidence in environmental policies.[65] At a European level, Directive 90/313/EEC on freedom of access to information on the environment, implemented in the United Kingdom by the Environmental Information Regulations 1992, is designed

---

[60] See eg Smith, Collar & Poustie, *Pollution Control in Scotland* (T&T Clark, 1997), ch 4.
[61] See eg Burton, 'Access to Environmental Information: the UK Experience of Water Registers' [1989] 1 JEL 192; Sanders & Rothnie, 'Planning Registers—Their Role in Promoting Public Participation' [1996] JPL 539.
[62] SI 1992/3240 as amended by SI 1998/1447. Other areas such as non-statutory corporate reporting requirements and product labelling are not considered for reasons of space.
[63] See eg Rivers (Prevention of Pollution) Act 1961, s 12.
[64] See Bell, *Ball & Bell on Environmental Law* (4th edn, Blackstone Press, 1997) p 157.
[65] 'This Common Inheritance', note 13 above, para 1.20.

partially to eliminate possible disparities in competition caused by differing laws on provision of environmental information and to improve environmental protection by involving citizens through information provision held by member states.[66] It should be noted that the Directive does not apply to the EU institutions themselves. Access to information at European Union level is considered further below. Finally, it should be noted that domestic initiatives in this area are underpinned by a number of international initiatives.[67]

Public registers

A very considerable amount of planning and environmental information is held on public registers. Registers are held by a variety of bodies including the Scottish Environment Protection Agency ('SEPA'),[68] local authorities[69] and the Scottish Ministers.[70] The establishment of SEPA in 1996 and the consequent reduction in the number of environmental regulators has led to a concentration of environmental registers. This should result in a number of benefits including the replacement of a variety of administrative practices by a single set of administrative practices, the availability of multiple registers at single contact points and the standardisation of charges for copies from the registers.[71]

Although the information held on registers varies from one legislative regime to another, broadly such registers normally contain information on licence applications, copies of the actual licences with the conditions to which they are subject, details of any modifications to licences and details of any enforcement action taken against the licence holder.[72]

In all cases where registers are provided for, a duty is imposed on the register holder to establish the register and to afford provision for public inspection free of charge at reasonable times.[73] Register holders regard normal working hours as the reasonable time to allow access to public registers.

---

[66] [1990] OJ L158/56.
[67] Eg Rio Declaration on Environment and Development, 13 June 1992, UNCED, A/Conf/151/4, Principle 10. The FOI Act will need to take account of the UN Economic Commission for Europe Convention on access to information, public participation in decision-making and access to justice in environmental matters (the Aarhus Convention) 1998 which the UK signed in June 1998 (see 'Freedom of Information: Consultation on Draft Legislation', Cm 4355, May 1999, para 54).
[68] Eg on: integrated pollution control and local air pollution control authorisations (Environmental Protection Act 1990 (EPA 1990), s 20), water quality objectives and discharge consents (Control of Pollution Act 1974 (COPA 1974), s 41), waste management licences (EPA 1990 s 64), and radioactive waste accumulation and disposal authorisations (Radioactive Substances Act 1993 (RSA 1993), s 39).
[69] Eg on: planning applications and decisions (Town and Country Planning (Scotland) Act 1997, s 36), hazardous substances consents (Planning (Hazardous Substances) (Scotland) Act 1997, s 27), and measurements taken in noise abatement zones (COPA, Part III; Noise Level (Measurement and Registers) (Scotland) Regulations 1982).
[70] Eg on licences granted in relation to dumping and incineration of waste at sea under the Food and Environment Protection Act 1985.
[71] See eg SEPA, 'Guide to Environmental Information Available to the Public', Smith, Collar & Poustie, op cit, note 59 above, p 68.
[72] See eg EPA 1990, s 20; Environmental Protection (Applications, Appeals and Registers) Regulations 1991 (SI 1991/507 as amended), regs 15–17.
[73] Eg EPA 1990, s 20(1) and (7).

Unfortunately research reveals that such an approach may not be adequate.[74] There is no need to show a particular interest to obtain access to the information and any member of the public may inspect the registers regardless of his or her motive for doing so.[75] Generally, reasonable charges may be levied for copies from the registers but no fee may be levied for inspection of the register.[76] Prior to the establishment of SEPA there was widespread variation in the charges applied.[77] Since the introduction of the Environmental Information Regulations 1992 it has become possible to request copies of information held on a register by letter, telephone, fax or in some cases by e-mail, which may help to overcome some of the problems of restricted opening hours.[78] SEPA has also indicated that it is endeavouring to develop on-line information provision.[79] If this were to be extended to registers it would enhance their accessibility considerably.

In most cases information may be excluded from the registers on two grounds: (1) national security[80] and (2) commercial confidentiality.[81] A mere claim that information is commercially confidential is not sufficient: the register holder, or the Scottish Ministers on appeal,[82] must make a determination to that effect otherwise the information will be included on the register.

One register which received considerable publicity was the Chemical Releases Inventory ('CRI'). The CRI was a non-statutory register developed by Her Majesty's Inspectorate of Pollution (now part of the Environment Agency) providing extensive although incomplete information about emissions from the various integrated pollution control processes operating in England and Wales. The CRI's wider exposure resulted from its publication by Friends of the Earth on the internet.[83] This is an interesting example of an interest group acting as an information broker, making available government information more accessible than it otherwise would be. However, the CRI was not kept up to date and some emissions data were not published at all. Recently the CRI has been relaunched as the Pollution Inventory ('PI'), which contains 1998 emissions data for all integrated pollution control processes in England and Wales.[84] The CRI and the PI foreshadow the requirement in Article 15(3) of

---

[74] See eg Sanders & Rothnie, op cit, note 60 above, p 543. On-line access may be a partial solution, although not everyone has access to a computer.
[75] *Stirrat Park Hogg* v *Dumbarton District Council* 1996 SLT 1113, 1994 SCLR 631.
[76] Ibid.
[77] Scottish Consumer Council and Friends of the Earth Scotland, 'Come clean! Public access to information about local authority air pollution control', March 1993. This report identified a range of charges between 5p and £5 per page for photocopies from local air pollution control registers.
[78] This is the effect of Environmental Information Regulations 1992, reg 5.
[79] See eg SEPA, 'Corporate Plan 1999–2000', April 1999, p 39.
[80] EPA 1990, ss 21, 65 and 78S; COPA 1974, s 42A; and RSA 1993, s 39.
[81] EPA 1990, ss 22, 66 and 78T; and COPA 1974, s 42B. In the case of RSA 1993 information may be excluded from the register where it would otherwise involve the disclosure of a trade secret (s 39).
[82] Given that national security and commercial confidentiality both raise non-devolved issues, the appeal functions are exercisable by the Scottish Ministers only after consultation with the Secretary of State: the Scotland Act 1998 (Transfer of Functions to the Scottish Ministers etc) Order 1999 (SI 1999/1750), Art 3 and Sched 2. The Secretary of State also has a concurrent right to determine such appeals (ibid), but one would assume that in practice this would normally be left to the Scottish Ministers.
[83] http://www.foe.uk/cri/index.html.
[84] See 'Pollution Inventory redraws the map for environmental information' [1999] 292 ENDS Report 24. The Pollution Inventory is available on-line at http://www.environment-agency.gov.uk/.

Directive 96/61/EC on integrated pollution prevention and control which requires the EC Commission to publish an inventory, based on data to be provided by member states of the principal emissions and the sources responsible every three years.[85] The implementing legislation in the United Kingdom, the Pollution Prevention and Control Act 1999, enables regulations to be made requiring the compilation and provision of information on emissions.[86] The PI would presumably form the basis of the information to be supplied to the Commission. No Scottish version of the CRI or PI has been developed although implementation of Directive 96/61/EC will presumably require this.

The Environmental Information Regulations 1992

The Environmental Information Regulations 1992 ('the 1992 Regulations') are designed to implement Directive 90/313/EEC on the freedom of access to information on the environment. The core provision is that any 'relevant person' who holds any 'information that relates to the environment' to which the 1992 Regulations apply must make that information available to every person who requests it (regulation 3(1)).

'Information that relates to the environment' is fairly widely defined (regulation 2(2))[87] and includes anything held in records, reports and returns, as well as computer records and other non-documentary records (regulation 2(4)). The information must not be held for the purposes of any judicial or legislative function and it must be neither information which is required by statute to be provided on request nor information contained in records which must be made available for public inspection (regulation 2(1)(c)). This means that the principal obligation does not extend to information held on registers. However, as noted above, to ensure that arrangements for existing statutory rights to information comply with the requirements of the 1992 Regulations, such arrangements must provide that every request is dealt with in the same way as a request under the Regulations would be (regulation 5).

'Relevant persons' are defined as:

'(a) all such Ministers of the Crown, Government departments, local authorities and other persons carrying out functions of public administration at a national, regional or local level as, for the purposes of or in connection with their functions, have responsibilities in relation to the environment; and

---

[85] OJ L257/26, 24.9.96.
[86] Separate regulations are being made for Scotland: Scottish Executive, 'Final Consultation on Draft Pollution Prevention and Control (Scotland) Regulations 2000, (2000), which contains the draft regulations.
[87] The presence of dumped naval munitions in a disused mineshaft was information relating to the state of land in terms of reg 2(2)(a): *R v British Coal Corporation, ex Ibstock Building Products Ltd* [1995] Env LR 277 which also established that the source of information is capable of being information that relates to the environment because it is necessary to know the source of the information to assess its quality and credibility. See also *Mecklenburg v Kreis Pinneberg* C-321/96 [1998] 10 ELM 252.

(b) any body with public responsibilities for the environment which does not fall within sub-paragraph (a) above but is under the control of a person falling within that sub-paragraph.' (reg 2(3)).

Although, as part of the consultation process prior to the introduction of the 1992 Regulations, the then Government published an indicative list of more than 200 bodies which it believed would be subject to the Regulations, it ultimately decided against providing a definitive list since it would change rapidly.[88] Bodies were also advised that they must decide whether or not they are subject to the 1992 Regulations.[89] This effectively puts the onus of establishing that a particular body is subject to the 1992 Regulations on the person seeking the information through judicial review proceedings, which seems to be against the spirit of openness lying behind the Regulations.[90] In line with the proposals in the Labour administration's White Paper 'Your Right to Know' the FOI Bill contains such a list (and certain exceptions) together with a power to designate further bodies by order, but similar problems may no doubt arise and it might well be easier to include a list of bodies that are *not* subject to the FOI regime.

While the first category of bodies in the definition is relatively uncontroversial the scope of the second category of persons is much less clear. It appears possible that utilities may fall within the second category since the test is similar although not identical to the test of whether a person is a branch of the state for the purposes of establishing the EC principle of direct effect.[91] The House of Lords has been critical of the uncertainty surrounding whether or not utilities are subject to the 1992 Regulations.[92] The Government's own guidance notes that 'control' is a relationship constituted by statutes, rights, contracts or other means which confer the possibility of exercising a decisive influence on a body.

Importantly, a person does not need to demonstrate any interest in the information concerned. The 1992 Regulations provide a skeleton framework of arrangements in relation to disclosure of information and, as a result of this, different public authorities have adopted detailed arrangements which vary considerably. However, relevant persons must respond to requests for information as soon as possible and not more than two months after the request was made (regulation 3(2)). It is not yet clear whether a holding letter within the two-month period would constitute a valid response. A refusal to make information available must be in writing and must specify reasons for the refusal (regulation

---

[88] 'Guidance on the Implementation of the Environmental Information Regulations 1992' (DoE, 1992).
[89] Ibid. For example, BNFL unsurprisingly has taken the view that it is not subject to the 1992 Regulations despite its inclusion on the then Government's indicative list of bodies covered: Frankel & Ecclestone, 'The Environmental Information Regulations and THORP' (December 1993) paras 3.1 and 7.1.
[90] This approach was strongly criticised in 'Freedom of Access to Information on the Environment', House of Lords' Select Committee on the European Communities, First Report, Session 1996–97, HL Paper 9.
[91] Control through regulation is one of the key elements in establishing that a body is an emanation of the state for the purposes of direct effect, see eg *Foster v British Gas* C-188/89 [1991] 2 AC 306; *Griffin v South West Water Services* [1995] IRLR 15. Bakkenist argues for an even wider interpretation, ie that every person possessing an environmental licence falls within the second category: *Environmental Information: Law, Policy & Experience*, (Cameron May, 1994) pp 60–63.
[92] See 'Freedom of Access to Information on the Environment', note 89 above.

3(2)).⁹³ Costs reasonably attributable to the supply of information may be charged (regulation 3(4)).⁹⁴ There is no doubt that charges may act as potential barriers to access to information.⁹⁵ Information need only be made available in such form and at such times and places as may be reasonable (regulation 3(5)). This is likely to be interpreted as meaning during normal working hours. However, given that information may be requested by letter, telephone etc, this problem is ameliorated to some extent.

It is only possible to restrict disclosure on grounds which are consistent with the grounds set out in the 1992 Regulations (regulation 3(7)). The grounds for non-disclosure which a member state might employ are exhaustively set out in Article 3 of the Directive although a member state need not adopt all the grounds. Perhaps unsurprisingly the then Government chose to implement all nine available grounds for non-disclosure in the 1992 Regulations (regulation 4). This restrictive approach may also be seen at work in the 'UK Code of Practice'. In some cases the relevant person may treat the information as confidential such as where it relates to international relations, national defence or public security,⁹⁶ or legal proceedings,⁹⁷ or confidential internal deliberations, or is contained in unfinished records,⁹⁸ or is commercially confidential. In other cases, including if the disclosure would result in a statutory requirement or agreement being breached, or if it is personal information contained in records held in relation to an individual who has not consented to its disclosure,⁹⁹ or the disclosure would increase the likelihood of damage to the environment, the information must be treated as confidential and not disclosed.

In addition, a request for information may be refused in cases where the request is manifestly unreasonable or is formulated in too general a manner (regulation 3(3)). This is a catch-22 provision, as it appears to require knowledge of exactly what information is held in relation to a particular issue.

Where information can be separated from information that is confidential, it must be disclosed (regulation 4(4)).

Article 4 of Directive 90/313/EEC provides that a person may seek a judicial or administrative review of an adverse decision in accordance with the relevant national legal system. The 1992 Regulations do not make any express reference to remedies for adverse decisions but it is clear that judicial review would be

---

⁹³ General case law on giving reasons indicates that the decision-maker must give proper and adequate reasons that deal with the substantial questions in an intelligible way, see eg *Wordie Property Co Ltd v Secretary of State for Scotland* 1984 SLT 345.
⁹⁴ See also the discussion of this issue in relation to information held on registers above on p 78.
⁹⁵ See 'Freedom of Access to Information on the Environment', note 89 above.
⁹⁶ In *R v British Coal Corporation, ex p Ibstock Building Products Ltd* [1995] Env LR 277 the presence of munitions allegedly dumped in mineshafts in 1947 was held not to be a matter which affected national defence or public security, especially as the Ministry of Defence did not take up the matter.
⁹⁷ The scope of this exemption has been clarified by *Mecklenburg v Kreis Pinneberg* C-321/96 [1998] 10 ELM 252 and the Environmental Information (Amendment) Regulations 1998 (SI 1998/1447). See also *R v British Coal Corporation, ex p Ibstock Building Products Ltd*, note 96 above.
⁹⁸ See *Maile v Wigan Metropolitan Borough Council* [1999] 294 ENDS Report 55 in which the High Court upheld the local authority's contention that a database of potentially contaminated sites in its area was information still in the course of completion.
⁹⁹ Information supplied by an individual in *R v British Coal Corporation, ex p Ibstock Building Products Ltd*, note 95 above, was not personal information contained in records held in relation to an individual who had not given his consent to its disclosure as the records were not held in relation to the individual informant.

available, for example, to establish that a body is a relevant person or to challenge unreasonable charges imposed for the supply of information. Given the costs involved in judicial review, it is not a particularly accessible remedy and is likely to be used only where considerable economic interests are at stake.[100] For aggrieved individuals an alternative remedy may be available through the offices of the United Kingdom Parliamentary Ombudsman, the Scottish Parliamentary Ombudsman or Local Ombudsman depending on whether the person refusing to supply information is a central or local government body. There is no obligation on relevant persons to establish an internal review procedure although subsequently the 'UK Code of Practice' recommended that complaints should first be directed to the government body concerned. To improve matters initially the Government proposed the establishment of a new tribunal to deal with complaints relating to environmental information.[101] However, the UK FOI Bill contains provisions for a UK Information Commissioner with a right of appeal to an Information Tribunal and a further appeal on points of law to the courts. Similar proposals for Scotland are contained in 'An Open Scotland' (paras 6.12–6.16).

Difficulties identified with current planning and environmental FOI provisions

Lack of awareness of the provisions has been identified as a serious problem, together with the accessibility of premises in which information is held in terms of location, opening hours and access for the disabled, the comprehensiveness, sufficiency and comprehensibility of data, the availability of staff assistance and the cost of making copies.[102]

Of charters and codes

Given that the Conservative administration was committed to making local government and the provision of public services by, for example, National Health Service Trusts, more accountable and transparent, it became less easy to defend central government secrecy. The Government therefore became committed to greater openness but principally only so long as this was a non-statutory right.[103] Since it accepted the need for statutory rights in the various fields discussed above the reason why a non-statutory right was best for access to other central

---

[100] Eg a large redevelopment project was involved in *R v British Coal Corporation, ex p Ibstock Building Products Ltd*, note 95 above.
[101] See eg 'Government promises appeals body for environmental information' [1997] 265 ENDS Report 35.
[102] See eg Burton, 'Access to Environmental Information: the UK Experience of Water Registers' [1989] 1 JEL 192; Scottish Consumer Council and Friends of the Earth Scotland, 'Come clean! Public access to information about local authority air pollution control', March 1993; John, 'Access to Environmental Information: Limitations of the UK Radioactive Substances Registers' [1995] 7 JEL 11; Rowan-Robinson, Ross, Walton & Rothnie, 'Public Access to Environmental Information: A Means to What End?' [1996] 8 JEL 19; Sanders & Rothnie, 'Planning Registers—Their Role in Promoting Public Participation' [1996] JPL 539; Reid, Lloyd, Illsey & Lynch, 'Effective Public Access to Planning Information' [1998] JPL 1028.
[103] See eg White Paper, 'Open Government', Cm 2290, July 1993.

government information was never convincingly explained. The Citizen's Charter was one of the initiatives in this area.

In its White Paper 'Open Government',[104] which was described as a development of the Citizen's Charter programme, the Conservative Government proposed the development of a 'Code of Practice on Access to Government Information' and this was subsequently implemented.[105] With the advent of devolution the Scottish Executive has adopted a very similar code (the 'Scottish Code of Practice').[106] The 'Scottish Code of Practice' is designed

- 'to facilitate policy-making and the democratic process by providing access to the facts and analyses which provide the basis for consideration of proposed policy;
- to protect the interests of individuals and companies by ensuring that reasons are given for administrative decisions, except where there is statutory authority or established convention to the contrary; ...'.[107]

Against these aims are balanced the need

- 'to maintain high standards of care in ensuring the privacy of personal and commercially confidential information; and
- to preserve confidentiality where disclosure would not be in the public interest or would breach personal privacy or the confidences of a third party in accordance with statutory requirements and Part II of the Code.'[108]

The UK and Scottish Codes of Practice (the 'Codes') put far more emphasis on reasons for confidentiality than on positive access to information. There are no fewer than 15 categories of information which are exempt from the Codes' commitments.[109] These include defence, security and international relations, internal discussions and advice, law enforcement and legal proceedings, immigration and nationality and voluminous or vexatious requests. As 'Your Right to Know' recognised, the category-based approach to exemptions can certainly be criticised as being too broad. A contents-based approach would seem to be more open. It would also allow partial disclosure of a record. In most cases, there is a presumption in favour of disclosure subject to a harm test where the harm outweighs the public interest in disclosure. It should be noted that this is a

---

[104] Ibid. See also Birkinshaw, ' "I only ask for information"—the White Paper on open government' [1993] PL 557.
[105] 'Code of Practice on Access to Government Information' (2nd edn, 1997). The first edition is contained at Annex A of the White Paper, 'Open Government'.
[106] 'Code of Practice on Access to Scottish Executive Information', July 1999. See also Scottish Office News Release 1311/99, 23 June 1999.
[107] The UK Code of Practice has very similar although not identical aims: to improve policy-making and the democratic process by extending access to facts and analyses which provide the basis for consideration of proposed policy; to ensure that reasons are given for administrative decisions, except where there is statutory authority or established convention to the contrary; and to further the Citizen's Charter principles of public service.
[108] Scottish Code of Practice, Part I, para 2.
[109] This is more than any of the main statutory FOI regimes worldwide, see 'Your Right to Know', para 3.3 and Annex D.

simple harm test, much less stringent than the substantial harm test proposed in 'Your Right to Know'. What constitutes the public interest is also left undefined.

In addition to committing bodies to setting up internal review systems, the Codes provide a form of independent remedy through the offices of the Parliamentary Commissioner for Administration (the Ombudsman) and his Scottish counterpart. However, not all UK central government bodies are subject to the UK Ombudsman's jurisdiction: the Cabinet Office, the Prime Minister's Office, the Bank of England, GCHQ, SIS and the Security Service are not. The Scottish Ombudsman's jurisdiction only covers those areas of government devolved to the new Scottish institutions. Moreover, many subjects are outwith the Ombudsmen's jurisdiction including commercial and contractual matters, personnel matters, criminal and civil proceedings, international relations, extradition, and national security. The Ombudsmen also have no power of enforcement but may only make recommendations which need not be implemented by the public authority concerned.

A target timetable of supplying requested information within 20 days applies under both Codes although this may be extended and where a request is refused, an explanation will normally be given. This is considerably weaker than a duty to give reasons and removes the onus from the body concerned of explaining which of the many grounds for refusing access to information it is relying upon. It is left to government bodies to make their own arrangements for charges for supplying information. Inevitably widely varying charges have been adopted and in some cases these have been manifestly unreasonable.[110]

The limitations of the Codes should be readily apparent. In addition, the 'UK Code of Practice' has suffered from scant publicity and few resources.[111]

Active dissemination of information

There has been considerable progress in the active dissemination of information by Government which has been aided in no small measure by developments in information technology. For example, in the environmental sphere Article 7 of Directive 90/313/EEC requires member states to disseminate general information on the environment. To this end SEPA published a 'State of the Environment Report' in 1996.[112] Furthermore, Government action on the environment throughout the United Kingdom is also regularly publicised through the annual follow-up reports to the White Paper 'This Common Inheritance'[113] which indicate the extent to which earlier commitments are being met and also set new targets.

More generally, the development of the internet has enabled large quantities of information to be made available on-line by government. For example, the Scottish Executive website contains much valuable information ranging from daily press releases to consultation documents, published research reports and

---

[110] See Birkinshaw, op cit note 1 above, p 205.
[111] See eg ibid, p 210.
[112] See SEPA, 'State of the Environment' 1996 and also http://www.sepa.org.uk/ for an on-line version.
[113] Cm 1200, 1990.

guidance.[114] The Department of the Environment, Transport and the Regions website contains current and archive air quality monitoring information and drinking water quality information as well as consultation papers and much additional information.[115] As noted above even the Security Service and GCHQ have established informative websites.

THE GOVERNMENT'S PROPOSALS

Introduction

The new Labour administration published the White Paper 'Your Right to Know: The Government's proposals for a Freedom of Information Act' in December 1997.[116] Preparation of the White Paper involved consideration of statutory FOI regimes in a number of other countries including Australia, New Zealand, the USA, France and Canada. In May 1999 the Government published a further consultation paper[117] together with a draft FOI Bill, a version of which was making it through Parliament at the time of writing. As noted above the Scottish Executive has also now indicated that it will be promoting Scottish FOI legislation, and the consultation paper, 'An Open Scotland', was published in November 1999.

Public authorities covered by the proposed FOI Act

The White Paper indicated that the following bodies would be subject to the FOI Act:

- government departments and executive agencies;
- nationalised industries, public corporations and non-departmental public bodies;
- the National Health Service;
- the administrative functions of the courts and tribunals;
- the administrative functions of the police and police authorities;
- the armed forces;
- local authorities;
- local public bodies such as training and enterprise councils;
- schools, further education colleges and universities;
- public service broadcasters;
- private organisations insofar as they carry out statutory functions; and
- the privatised utilities.

The merits of such a list may be doubtful on one level as it would probably require regular amendment. A list of bodies not covered would be simpler.[118]

---

[114] http://www.scotland.gov.uk/.
[115] http://www.detr.gov.uk/.
[116] Cm 3818, 1997.
[117] 'Freedom of Information: Consultation on Draft Legislation', Cm 4355, May 1999.
[118] See Birkinshaw, op cit, note 1 above, p 178.

However, the relatively broad scope of the legislation proposed in 'Your Right to Know' appeared to solve some of the problems encountered with the definition of 'relevant persons' in the Environmental Information Regulations 1992. For example, there could be no doubt that BNFL, which does not consider itself bound by the 1992 Regulations,[119] would be covered. However, uncertainty would still persist in relation, for example, to private organisations insofar as they carry out statutory functions.[120] This is perhaps inevitable given the trend towards devolution of public administration to the private sector. Doubts also seem likely to arise in relation to utilities since not all the current utilities are formerly nationalised industries, for example, Transco, Cellnet, and Scotrail.[121]

Schedule 1 to the UK FOI Bill contains a UK list of public authorities which will be subject to the regime:

- government departments (information relating to the Security Service, Secret Intelligence Service, GCHQ and certain other bodies dealing with security matters is exempt from disclosure);
- the National Assembly for Wales (and the Northern Ireland Assembly);
- the armed forces (except the special forces and any unit required to assist GCHQ);
- the National Health Service in England, Wales and Northern Ireland;
- local government bodies in England, Wales and Northern Ireland;
- maintained schools and other educational institutions such as universities in England and Wales and Northern Ireland;
- the police in England and Wales; and
- a wide range of other public bodies and offices in England, Wales and Northern Ireland.

The exclusion of the security and intelligence services and special forces and the information which they provide along with information held about them by other bodies was envisaged by 'Your Right to Know' and is not surprising. However, the broad scope originally envisaged by 'Your Right to Know' has been eroded to an extent despite Government assurances to the contrary. In particular, there is now uncertainty about whether or not privatised utilities will be covered. Their subjection to the regime now appears to be dependent on the Secretary of State exercising his power to designate further public bodies by order. The consultation paper which accompanied the draft FOI Bill indicated that the Government's intention is to designate all non-departmental public bodies and all private organisations carrying out public functions although designation of the latter cannot proceed without prior consultation.[122] However, this creates scope for such organisations to lobby for exclusion from the regime which could be very damaging to the public perception of the effectiveness of the legislation. Although the Government argues that because the police are now to be fully covered by the legislation the scope of the legislation is wider than that imposed by 'Your Right

---

[119] See Frankel & Ecclestone, *The Environmental Information Regulations and Thorp* (Campaign for Freedom of Information, December 1993, para 7.1). This appears to be confirmed by the UK FOI Bill, which extends the definition of public authorities to cover publicly owned corporations.
[120] See Birkinshaw, op cit, note 1 above, p 178.
[121] Graham, 'Human Rights and Public Utilities' [1998] 9 ULR 52 at p 54.
[122] 'Freedom of Information: Consultation on Draft Legislation', Cm 4355, May 1999, para 39.

to Know'[123] this is a highly disingenuous claim given that the scope of the regime will be dependent on the willingness of the Secretary of State to designate further bodies.

'An Open Scotland' proposes that the Scottish FOI legislation would set out the categories of public authorities to which it applied. The consultation paper provides an illustration list of such authorites which mirrors the range of bodies covered by the UK FOI Bill. However, 'An Open Scotland' makes clear that UK Governments and the agencies together with cross border public authorities such as the Forestry Commission will be subject to the UK rather than the Scottish FOI regime.

Information or records covered by the proposed FOI Act

A weakness of the Codes is that they provide access to information rather than documents which provides scope for 'doctoring' the material and is inefficient as it may be cumbersome to edit material for provision to an applicant rather than just disclosing a document. The UK FOI Bill applies to information recorded in any form. This provision is meant to address the problem idenified above as well as ensuring that information in electronic storage is covered. The information must be in connection with the authority's public functions.

The UK Government has also proposed that 'public records', that is historical records currently available under the Public Records Acts 1958 and 1967, should be brought within the scope of the UK FOI Act. 'Your Right to Know' explains that this does not mean that the same access provisions which apply to current records under the FOI Act will also apply to historical records, but that the move towards a unified Act is to improve the public's right of access to historical records. The UK Government proposes that the current rule that records will only be released after 30 years will continue but that more records will be released before 30 years have elapsed. It is also proposed that the criteria for withholding records for longer than 30 years in certain cases will be reformulated. These proposals are implemented by Part VI of the UK FOI Bill.

'An Open Scotland' does not propose any alteration to the public record system in Scotland, which is largely governed by the Public Records (Scotland) Act 1937, and the 30 year rule will continue to apply. However, consultation on the relationship between the scottish FOI regime and the Scottish public record system will take place. The possibility of separate national archive legislation for Scotland is to be considered.

Duty to disseminate information

A positive duty to disclose certain information pro actively was proposed in 'Your Right to Know'. The Government has implemented this commitment in the draft FOI Bill with a duty being placed on public authorities to establish and maintain a publication scheme in relation to information held by them and to review it from time to time. The scheme is meant to be a guide to the authority's publications and policies, for example on charging for information. The scheme must be approved by the

---

[123] Ibid, para 40.

Information Commissioner who may refuse to approve it or subsequently revoke his approval. To demonstrate its commitment to active disclosure of information the Government published the background material to 'Your Right to Know'.[124] 'An Open Scotland' proposes a similar scheme for Scotland (paras 2.15 and 2.16).

Applications

The key provision of the legislation is that any person who requests a public authority for information is entitled to be informed by the authority whether it holds the information and to have the information communicated to him. There are, however, certain cases where the duty to confirm or deny the existence of the information does not arise. Furthermore, if the information is exempt from disclosure it need not be supplied. As is noted below, there are many grounds on which information may be exempt from disclosure.

There is no need for the applicant to demonstrate an interest. However, the applicant must supply the authority with enough information in order that it may identify and locate the information requested. If the applicant does not do this, the authority is not under a duty to confirm or deny the existence of the information or supply it. Although this may appear to give rise to the catch-22 type situation discussed above (at p 81) in relation to the Environmental Information Regulations 1992, the duty imposed on authorities adopt and maintain the publication schemes mentioned above should assist applicants in identifying whether or not an authority holds certain types of information.

A duty is imposed on the authority to comply with the above duties promptly and in any event within 20 working days from the receipt of the application. 'An Open Scotland' proposes a similer period for compliance with a request for information in Scotland (para 2.14). It should be noted that this is in line with the period currently provided for by the Codes (see above p 84).

If a fee is payable for the information, the authority must notify the applicant in writing. The Secretary of State is empowered to make regulations providing what fees, if any, are payable, the maximum payable and how fees are to be calculated. Where the applicant is notified that a fee is payable, the 20-day period is extended by the time taken by the applicant to pay. The applicant has three months to pay from the date on which the fees notice is given to him. If he fails to pay within that time, the authority need not supply the information. 'An Open Scotland' contains similar proposals.

The UK Government intends that the fee regulations will not allow an authority to charge more than 10 per cent of the marginal cost of locating and disclosing the information together with any reasonable costs for copying, postage etc.[125] The level is to be set at or below £10 (the charge for subject access under the Data Protection Act 1998) for most applications.[126] Where the disclosure is a discretionary one (see below), there would be discretion to charge a fee at a level that was reasonable in the circumstances.

---

[124] In line with the commitment in 'Your Right to Know', para 3.13. See 'Your Right to Know—Background Material' also available at http://www.homeoffice.gov.uk/foi/.
[125] 'Freedom of Information: Consultation on Draft Legislation', note 121 above, para 58.
[126] Ibid.

'An Open Scotland' convasses views on a range of proposals from a flat rate £10 fee to a discretionary 10 per cent of the marginal costs plus additional costs. It indicates that while while the Scottish Executive does not wish to deter genuine applicants, the system should deter vexations requests and be simple for applicants and for authorities to operate. Bearing in mind the evidence from research into planning and environmental registers discussed above (p 82), it seems likely that fees may act as a considerable barrier to the take-up of rights of access to information, and the current proposals do little to dispel such concerns.

One notable omission from both the UK Bill and the proposals set out in 'An Open Scotland' is a positive duty to assist applicants. Such a duty might have had a significant role in the interpretation of the legislation and had a powerful symbolic role in helping to encourage a change to more open culture. However, the UK FOI Bill and 'An Open Scotland' envisage a Code of Practice issued to the public authorities which might well include advice on giving positive assistance to applicants.

Determining whether or not to disclose

To control vexatious and unreasonable applications 'Your Right to Know' suggested that, while applications would normally progress to being assessed against the harm and public interest tests, nonetheless the Act ought to provide for a number of 'gateways' in which applications could be turned down at an earlier stage. These included:

- where the information has already been published and is still reasonably available;
- applications for material which is to be published;
- applications which are not sufficiently specific;
- large-scale 'fishing' applications.

If the request passed through the initial gateways mentioned above 'Your Right to Know' proposed that the public authority must then determine whether or not disclosure of the information would cause *substantial harm* (harm alone in one case) (emphasis added) to one of the following interests: (a) national security; defence and international relations; (b) law enforcement; (c) personal privacy; (d) commercial confidentiality; (e) the safety of the individual, the public and the environment; (f) information supplied in confidence; and (g) the integrity of the decision-making and policy advice processes in government. This would have meant a welcome reduction from fifteen in the 'UK Code of Practice' to seven in the proposed FOI Act.

As was noted previously the UK FOI Bill provides that applications for UK information must be reasonably specific otherwise the authority need not confirm or deny the existence of the information or supply it. In addition, authorities' duties in relation to information are not triggered by vexatious requests or by repeat applications from the same person unless a reasonable interval has elapsed between the requests. The other former 'gateways' have now become exemptions. In addition, an authority's duties are not triggered where the cost of complying with a request exceeds 'the appropriate limit' which the Secretary of State may provide by regulations. The UK Government is apparently minded to set this limit at £500.[127] A similar approach is adopted in 'An Open Scotland' (paras 2.12 and 2.13; Chapter 4 and Annex C).

Even allowing for two of the former 'gateway' provisions being subsumed as exemptions, the list of exemptions has become somewhat daunting in the draft FOI Bill. Furthermore, the Government has backed away from the 'substantial harm' test proposed in 'Your Right to Know' and has arguably weakened the proposed legislation very considerably. The draft FOI Bill now provides that information will be exempt from disclosure if:

- it is reasonably accessible (even if payment is required) by other means;
- it is intended for future publication;
- it is supplied by or relating to the work of the security and intelligence services;
- its exemption is required for the purpose of safeguarding national security;
- its disclosure would or would be likely to prejudice defence or the capability or effectiveness of the armed forces;
- its disclosure would be or would be likely to prejudice relations between the United Kingdom and any other state;
- its disclosure would be or would be likely to prejudice relations between the UK government, the Scottish administration, the Executive Committee of the Northern Ireland Assembly or the National Assembly for Wales;
- its disclosure would be or would be likely to prejudice the economic interests of the United Kingdom or the financial interests of the UK government, the Scottish administration, the Executive Committee of the Northern Ireland Assembly or the National Assembly for Wales;
- it is information held for the purpose of any criminal or other investigation or criminal or civil proceedings arising out of an investigation;
- its disclosure would be or would be likely to prejudice law enforcement;
- it is held only by virtue of being contained in court records;
- it relates to the formulation or development of government policy and decision-making;
- it relates to communications with Her Majesty the Queen, the royal family or household or honours;
- its disclosure would or would be likely to endanger the physical or mental health of any individual or endanger the safety of any individual;
- it constitutes personal data of which the applicant is the data subject;
- it is information provided in confidence;
- it is subject to legal professional privilege;
- it constitutes a trade secret or if its disclosure would or would be likely to prejudice the commercial interests of any person; and
- its disclosure is prohibited by any other enactment or is incompatible with any EC obligation or would constitute or be punishable as a contempt of court.

A power is given to the Secretary of State to exempt further information by order. It will be apparent that certain information is now to be exempt from

---

[127] 'Freedom of Information: Consuiltation on Draft Legislation', note 121 above, para 59.

disclosure regardless of what degree of harm its disclosure might cause. Furthermore, the 'substantial harm' test has been replaced by a much weaker 'prejudice' test. The UK Government explains this watering down thus:

> '35. ... After further careful consideration our view is that a single omnibus substantial harm test cannot work properly for the range of separate exemptions proposed. What is "substantial" in relation to law enforcement, for example, may not be in relation to international relations. We consider that therefore the harm concerned must be capable of being interpreted clearly in line with the exemption in question. Where national security is an issue, for example, the test proposed is whether the exemption is required for the purpose of safeguarding national security. Where the health and safety of an individual is at issue, the test proposed is whether disclosure "would, or would be likely to endanger the physical or mental health or safety of an individual". Elsewhere the test is whether disclosure "would, or would be likely to prejudice" matters set out in the exemption in question.
>
> 36. The test proposed will result in a more open regime than under the existing Code of Practice in each of the areas in which it applies. The Code looks to the possibility of harm being caused: the test is risk, or reasonable expectation of prejudice, or whether disclosure could prejudice (for example) law enforcement. Under the provisions in the Bill the test is one of probability: would, or would be likely to prejudice. Thus the Bill will, of itself, lead to greater openness. The information Commissioner will be given the power to substitute his judgement for that of the public authority (as is currently the situation with regard to "the Ombudsman" and the Code). In this way the Commissioner will ensure that public authorities will be unsuccessful if they try to claim that prejudice will be caused in circumstances where the prejudice is trivial or frivolous. The prejudice must be real, actual or "of substance".
>
> 37. In one area, policy advice and the decision-taking process in central Government, the White Paper proposed a simple harm test, reflecting the need for public authorities to have time and space to formulate and develop new policies. There was no expectation that Freedom of Information legislation would lead to disclosure of Cabinet papers and minutes, law officers' advice, inter-Ministerial correspondence on developing policy, or information about the operation of a Minister's private office. The Bill puts it beyond doubt by creating a class exemption for this kind of information in clause 28(1) in place of the simple harm test. The latter would have created potential uncertainty and costs without extending access.
>
> 38. For the same reason other areas of policy development are covered in the Bill by an exemption based on the reasonable opinion of a Minister (or other qualified person) that disclosure would, or would be likely to prejudice the policy-making or decision-taking process. . . .'[128]

The reasoning behind this substantial policy shift appears flimsy at best. It is not at all clear that the 'prejudice' test envisaged in most exemptions is actually stronger than the test currently applied in the Codes. Furthermore, in relation to

---

[128] 'Freedom of Information: Consuiltation on Draft Legislation', note 121 above, paras 35–38.

access to information about policy formulation and development, there are now some examples of such information which are being publicised without causing harm and indeed which may serve to enhance debate, for example, the minutes of meetings between the Governor of the Bank of England and the Chancellor of the Exchequer.[129] To its credit, 'An Open Scotland' proposes that the harm test used in the various exemptions should involve consideration of whether the disclosure would or could be likely to substantially prejudice the interests protected (para 4.10 – 4.12).

The UK Government, however, also proposed in 'Your Right to Know' that even if the information was exempt from disclosure, a public interest test should be applied on a case-by-case basis to determine whether information should nonetheless be disclosed. This proposal has been partially implemented in the UK FOI Bill which obliges public authorities to consider disclosing certain information which would otherwise be exempt. In reaching a decision as to whether to disclose, authorities must consider whether in all the circumstances of the case, the public interest in disclosing the information outweighs the public interest in maintaining the exemption. Provision is made for charging fees for such information.

Where an authority refuses to disclose information because the request relates to exempt information, it must so notify the applicant and specify the applicable exemption(s) within the stipulated period. Where the authority has decided not to exercise its discretion to disclose otherwise exempt information in the public interest or has not reached a decision on that issue, it must so notify the applicant. Where an authority seeks to refuse a request on the basis that complying with it would exceed the limit set in regulations or that the application is vexatious etc, it must so notify the applicant within the time limits set down (see above pp 74–75).

Relationship with existing legislation

The UK Government has also indicated that it intends to repeal or amend the various provisions governing disclosure in other legislation. This may lead, for example, to the repeal of the Environmental Information Regulations 1992.[130]

The Government is proposing to replace as many of the existing provisions on access to personal information as possible.[131] However, the relationship of the FOI Act to the Data Protection Act 1998 is more complex (see above at p 74–75).

---

[129] A more local example is that of SEPA which publicises agendas and minutes of its main board meetings and generally permits public access to these. See http://www.sepa.org.uk/.

[130] 'Freedom of Information: Consultation on Draft Legislation', note 121 above, para 54 although the UK's signature of the UNECE Convention on access to information, public participation in decision-making and access to justice in environmental matters (the Aarhus Convention) 1998 may require modification to the general right to access to information in relation to environmental matters. This is reflected in the UK FOI Bill which permits the Secretary of State to make regulations implementing the Aarhus Convention. Environmental information would then be availble under those regulations and would be exempt from disclosure under the UK FOI regime.

[131] See pp 73–76 above for a brief discussion of existing provisions on access to personal information.

Oversight and enforcement[132]

An effective system of oversight and enforcement is essential to any FOI regime since it is that system which will ultimately guarantee the right to information. 'Your Right to Know' recognised the importance of a readily available, freely accessible, quick and effective review and appeal system.

'Your Right to Know' built on the provisions of the 'UK Code of Practice' by proposing the establishment of a new independent Information Commissioner to replace the Ombudsman's oversight and enforcement role under the Code. Although a UK Information Commissioner is established by the UK FOI Bill, in a departure from 'Your Right to Know', the UK Government has sensibly decided to merge the roles of the Data Protection Commissioner and the UK Information Commissioner. The rationale for this move is explained thus:

> '45. A significant number of requests for information are likely to be for a mixture of personal and more general information and authorities will have to make arrangements for co-ordinating such requests. It would be illogical for this not also to be reflected in the enforcement arrangements. The Government believes that a combined Commissioner for information and data protection is the most efficient and effective arrangement, and the one which will deliver a consistent application of the necessary balance between personal privacy and freedom of information.'[133]

The general functions of the UK Commissioner include the promotion of good practice by public authorities particularly by ensuring that they observe the requirements of the FOI legislation, their own publication schemes and any codes of practice issued by the Secretary of State. Where it appears to the UK Commissioner that the practice of an authority does not conform to the codes of practice or its own publication scheme he may serve a notice called a 'practice recommendation' on the authority specifying the steps which the authority should take to bring its practice into conformity.

The UK Commissioner may arrange for dissemination of information to the public about the operation of the legislation, which will be particularly important in terms of ensuring public awareness and understanding of the legislation, that the full potential for utilising the legislation is realised and that its relationship with the data protection regime is understood. The UK Commissioner must also report to Parliament annually on the exercise of his functions.

'Your Right to Know' envisaged a two-stage enforcement process.[134] First, a dissatisfied applicant would utilise an internal review procedure. If he was dissatisfied with the outcome of that review there would then be the possibility of appeal to the Information Commissioner. Although no statutory appeal to the courts was to be provided thereafter, judicial review of the Commissioner's

---

[132] See generally 'Freedom of Information: Consultation on Draft Legislation', note 121 above, paras 41–47.
[133] Ibid, para 45.
[134] See 'Your Right to Know', paras 5.1–5.19. 'An Open Scotland' contains similar proposals and seeks views on whether a Scottish Information Tribunal should be established to create a three-stage process (paras 6.12–6.16). It is not yet clear whether or not the internal review stage is to be on a statutory basis.

decision would have been possible as a third stage in the process. Failure to comply with the Commissioner's decisions was to be treated as contempt of court.

The enforcement provisions of the UK FOI Bill differ significantly from the original proposals. First, whereas 'Your Right to Know' proposed the formalisation of the internal review procedures, the UK FOI Bill does not require public authorities to set up an internal review procedure. Instead the proposed code of practice to be issued under the legislation is to set out good practice including the establishment of a complaints procedure within each public authority.[135] Then, in line with the proposals in 'Your Right to Know' the UK FOI Bill provides for an appeal ('application') to the UK Commissioner. This application can be made direct to the UK Commissioner, who will issue a decision notice. The Commissioner may, for example, determine whether or not an exemption applies or whether or not a charge levied for the supply of information is excessive. Although in general public authorities must comply with decision notices, Ministers may override such notices where they relate to decisions by the UK Commisioner to order disclosure in the public interest where an exemption nonetheless applies. This provision has understandably been the subject of much criticism, and it is welcome that 'An Open Scotland' proposes a narrower role for Ministerial Certificates in such cases (para 6.5) than the UK FOI Bill. In a departure from 'Your Right to Know', the draft FOI Bill provides for a further tier of appeal to the UK Information Tribunal (formerly the Data Protection Tribunal) by the complainant or the public authority. Both the UK Commissioner and the Tribunal may substitute their own decisions for that of the public authority or UK Commissioner as the case may be. From the Tribunal a further right of appeal on points of law lies to the Court of Session or to the High Court as appropriate.

In line with the proposals in 'Your Right to Know' the UK Commissioner need not deal with an application if the complainant has not exhausted the relevant public authority's complaints procedure. He may also decline to deal with late, frivolous or vexatious applications or applications that have been withdrawn or abandoned. However, where the UK Commissioner deals with a valid application and decides that a public authority has failed to comply with the requirements of the Act, he must serve a decision notice on it specifying the steps the authority must take to comply together with a timescale for compliance.

To assist him in his oversight and enforcement functions and to further an investigation the UK Commissioner is empowered to issue information notices requiring an authority to supply such information as he may specify. Considerable powers of inspection and entry are also given to the UK Commissioner. 'An Open Scotland' indicates that the Scottish Executive is proposing similar powers for the Scottish Commissioner.

A more general enforcement mechanism (which is not dependent on an appeal by a complainant) is provided in the form of an enforcement notice which the UK Commissioner may serve on an authority if he is satisfied that it has failed to comply with any requirements of the legislation. The notice must specify what steps need to be taken to comply with those requirements and must also set out the authority's right of appeal to the Tribunal. An appeal suspends the operation of the notice pending its determination or withdrawal.

If a public authority fails to comply with a decision notice, an information

---

[135] 'Freedom of Information: Consultation on Draft Legislation', note 121 above, para 42.

notice or an enforcement notice the UK Commissioner may certify that fact to the Court of Session in Scotland or High Court in England, Wales or Northern Ireland and the court may, after hearing evidence, deal with the matter as if it were a contempt of court.

The Commissioner may also seek to resolve disputes by informal methods as 'Your Right to Know' proposed when it envisaged the UK Commissioner being given the right to resolve disputes by mediation.[136] Although no such formal power is given to the UK Commissioner, there would appear to be nothing to prevent him from using such dispute resolution methods.

A very welcome proposal in 'Your Right to Know' was that there were to be no provision for a ministerial veto or certificate permitting interference with appeal decisions or overriding the Commissioner's decisions. The UK Government commendably took the view that such a veto would undermine the authority of the Information Commissioner and erode public confidence in the FOI Act. In the UK FOI Bill there are provisions for ministerial certificates which are to be conclusive proof that information relates to the work of the security and intelligence services or national security and is thus exempt. Yet, the legislation also provides for appeals against such a certificate by the Commissioner or any applicant whose request for information is affected by the issue of the certificate. It is welcome that such certificates will not simply have the force of a *fiat*. However, diappointingly, no appeal is available in relation to a Ministerial Certificate which has been issued to override the UK Commissioner's decision that information should be disclosed in the public interest where an exemption applies.

Bringing about a culture change

Both the UK Government and the Scottish Executive recognise that legislation will not in itself result in greater openness but that openness needs to be championed within government to ensure that there is a genuine culture change. An FOI Unit has been set up in the Cabinet Office to promote a culture of openness. The role of the UK and Scottish Commissioners discussed above will undoubtedly assist in promoting the FOI Act. A number of positive suggestions are made in 'Your Right to Know' and 'An Open Scotland' to develop an FOI culture including a guide for the public on using the FOI Act, guidance for public authorities on the FOI Act and training for officers in public authorities.

ACCESS TO INFORMATION AT EU LEVEL

It is somewhat ironic that, at the very time we appear to be on the verge of developing a comprehensive freedom of information regime in the United Kingdom, the lack of transparency of the EU institutions has become a key issue. With the transfer of decision-making power in a wide range of areas from member states to

---

[136] 'Your Right to Know', para 5.12. 'An Open Scotland' envisages formal powers to resolve disputes by mediation for Scottish Commissioner (para 6.5).

the EU institutions, the need for more transparency is clear.[137] However, the attitude of the Council and Commission to access to information remains strikingly reminiscent of the long-standing UK tradition of secrecy.

Transparency only became a significant issue for member states in the run-up to the Maastricht Treaty.[138] In the event only a declaration was attached to the Maastricht Treaty noting that the public's confidence in the administration would be strengthened by transparency and recommending that the Commission should report to the Council no later than 1993 on measures designed to improve public access to information held by the institutions. As a result the Commission adopted two communications on public access to documents and openness. This was followed by the adoption by the Council and Commission of a 'Code of Conduct concerning Public Access to Council and Commission documents' which was implemented by decisions.[139] The governing principle of the Code is that 'The public will have the widest possible access to documents held by the Commission and Council'. However, various exceptions, some mandatory and some discretionary, are set out. The mandatory exceptions include protection of the public interest (public security, international relations, monetary stability, court proceedings, inspections and investigations), the protection of the individual and privacy, the protection of commercial and industrial secrecy. The discretionary ground may be used to protect the institution's interest in the confidentiality of its proceedings.

Although the 'Code of Conduct' is essentially a series of voluntary obligations that the Commission has undertaken, it nevertheless is capable of conferring legal rights on third parties which the Commission is obliged to respect.[140] The exceptions must be construed and applied strictly so that the objective of transparency is not rendered unattainable.[141] Although the exception relating to the opening of proceedings under Article 226 of the EC Treaty as amended is mandatory, if documents relating to such proceedings are requested, in refusing the request the Commission must nevertheless indicate the reasons why it considers that the documents relate to possible Article 226 proceedings, their subject matter and the inspections or investigations they might involve.[142] Where the Commission failed to give reasons why requested documents related to possible Article 226 proceedings and failed to balance the relevant interests involved, their decision violated Article 253 of the EC Treaty as amended and was accordingly annulled.[143]

The cases highlight the failure of EU institutions to pay adequate regard to the issue of access to information. Given that it is clear that the minimal rights that do exist rely on unilateral obligations, rather than a fundamental right, it appears that

---

[137] See eg Curtin & Meijers, 'The Principle of Open Government in Schengen and the European Union: Democratic Retrogression?' [1995] 32 CMLRev 391.
[138] The Dutch unsuccessfully sought to have a provision included in the treaty on the subject to allow the Council to adopt a Regulation in relation to access to information held by the EC institutions.
[139] 'Code of Conduct concerning public access to Council and Commission documents' OJ [1993] L340/41 implemented by Council Decision 93/731 on public access to Council documents OJ L340/43 and Commission Decision 94/90/ECSC, EC, Euratom on public access to Commission documents, OJ [1994] L46/58, 18.2.94.
[140] *WWF UK v EC Commission* (T-105/95) [1997] All ER (EC) 300, ECR II-313, [1997] 9 ELM 113.
[141] Ibid.
[142] Ibid.
[143] Ibid.

access to information is regarded very much as a mere administrative concession.¹⁴⁴ The court cases that have been brought highlight the extremely limited nature of the right of access to information at EU level and show up starkly the failure to live up to the declaration in the Maastricht Treaty on European Union. In that sense the cases may assist with the evolution of the right.¹⁴⁵ It has been pointed out that existing remedies for refusal of access to information at EU level are also prohibitively expensive.¹⁴⁶ The only successful cases so far have been brought by a major British newspaper and a leading international environmental interest group.¹⁴⁷

CONCLUSIONS—PARADISE POSTPONED?

The UK Government's proposals for an FOI Act in 'Your Right to Know' were well designed and, if implemented, would certainly have helped to advance a culture of greater openness and accountability in government. However, the UK FOI Bill is markedly weaker than the legislation envisaged in 'Your Right to Know' in that a large number of exemptions involving a weaker harm test are to apply and as the UK Commissioner's decisions to order disclosure in the public interst may be overriden by Ministers. Although the final shape of the Scottish Executive's proposals is not yet clear, it is apparent from 'An Open Scotland' that the weaknesses of the UK FOI Bill may be avoided. However, there is still time for the Scottish proposals to be watered down. One downside of the devolution arrangements is that with the prospect of separate UK and Scottish FOI legislation, confusion will arise in the minds of the public as to which legislation is applicable to particular information, quite apart from the possibility of different access rights and appeal mechanisms. A fragmented FOI system might well hamper the cause of greater openness although one can also envisage that if stronger Scottish FOI legislation is enacted, it may well give rise to calls for a similar system south of the border.

---

¹⁴⁴ See O'Neill, 'In search of a real right of access to EC-held documentation' [1997] PL 446 at pp 452–453.
¹⁴⁵ Ibid. See also Chiti, 'The Right of Access to Community Information under the Code of Practice: the Applications for Administrative Development' [1996] 2 EPL 363.
¹⁴⁶ O'Neill, op cit, p 453.
¹⁴⁷ *Carvel v Council of the European Union* (T 194/94) [1996] All ER (EC) 53, [1995] 3 CMLR 359; and *WWF UK v EC Commission* (T-105/95), note 139 above. On the *Carvel* case, see Campbell, 'Access to European Community Official Information' (1997) 46 ICLQ 174.

6: SCOTTISH CRIMINAL JUSTICE AND THE HUMAN RIGHTS ACT

Christopher Gane

INTRODUCTION

It is often supposed that the main impact of the Human Rights Act will be in the field of criminal justice. The other chapters in this collection clearly demonstrate that this is not the case, and that the impact of the Act, especially when read along with the Scotland Act, is likely to be significant across most aspects of Scots law. Undoubtedly, however, the effect of the 'Convention rights' on our system of criminal justice is potentially very significant.

It is not possible, of course, in a chapter of this length, to examine all aspects of the criminal justice system and the extent to which the system as a whole, or individual features of it, are compatible with Convention rights. What this chapter concentrates on, therefore, are two salient features of our system of criminal justice, and the extent to which they may give rise to issues under the Human Rights Act. The first is the much-vaunted 'flexibility' of our criminal law (or, more specifically, the common law). The second is the very extensive degree of discretion exercised by the public prosecutor in Scotland and the very limited external controls over the exercise of that discretion. These topics have been selected because of their centrality to the whole of the criminal justice system, and for the potential effect of the Human Rights Act in these areas.

LEGALITY, FLEXIBILITY AND CONVENTION RIGHTS

To a marked degree, Scottish criminal law is dependent upon the common law for the definition of its major offences. While, in practice, much of the business of the courts, particularly the lower courts, concerns statutory offences (in particular road traffic and other regulatory offences), large areas of the law remain untouched by statute. Thus, most offences against the person and property are based upon the common law, as are the general principles of criminal liability and inchoate offences. In addition to these offences, the boundaries of which are reasonably well defined,[1] are categories of criminal conduct, such as 'causing real injury',[2]

---

[1] This is not to say, however, that these boundaries are fixed. Major changes do occur in the definition of apparently well-established offences. See, for example, the dramatic extension of malicious mischief discussed below. A further, more gradual change, is to be found in the disappearance of the 'requirement of an intention permanently to deprive' from the law of theft, achieved by judicial decision over a 20-year period, beginning with the decision of a sheriff in *Herron* v *Best* 1976 SLT (Sh Ct) 80, and concluding with the decision of the High Court in *Black* v *Carmichael, Carmichael* v *Black* 1992 SLT 897.

[2] ie causing personal injury.

'shameless indecency', and 'breach of the peace', the boundaries of which are considerably less certain.[3] Even where there are relevant statutory offences, Scottish prosecutors will often prefer to rely upon common law offences that are defined with significantly less precision (and in much simpler terms) than their statutory equivalents.

Reliance upon common law charges, the boundaries of which are not always clearly defined, naturally tends towards 'flexibility' in the system. This flexibility is enhanced by a procedural rule relating to the manner in which criminal charges are stated. In drawing up an indictment or summary complaint, it is not necessary for the prosecutor to specify by reference to any *nomen juris* the offence which is charged. It is sufficient if the charge sets out facts which, if proved, would constitute a criminal offence.[4] It is hardly surprising, then, that prosecutors faced with conduct which they consider to be socially harmful, take advantage of this provision to extend the criminal law. Challenges to criminal charges on the ground that the indictment does not reveal an offence known to the law are, understandably, quite frequently encountered in Scottish procedure.[5]

As suggested above, reliance on judicially developed crimes raises questions of fundamental importance, not only for the discipline of criminal law, but for society as a whole. Whether, in a democratic community, the responsibility for determining what should be punished as a crime should be entrusted to the courts and public prosecutors to the extent that this happens in Scotland is an issue of constitutional significance, and one which is brought sharply to the fore with the passing of the Human Rights Act. Concisely put, the question is this: to what extent is judicial development of the criminal law, as is practised in Scotland, compatible with the principle of legality, as enshrined in the European Convention on Human Rights?

The principle of legality in the European Convention

The principle of legality appears in two 'guises' in the European Convention on Human Rights. It is most explicitly stated in Article 7 of the Convention which provides as follows:

'(1) No one shall be held guilty of any criminal offence on account of any act or omission which did not constitute a criminal offence under national or international law at the time when it was committed. Nor shall a heavier penalty be imposed than the one that was applicable at the time the criminal offence was committed.

(2) This article shall not prejudice the trial and punishment of any person for any act or omission which, at the time when it was committed, was

---

[3] See below.
[4] Criminal Procedure (Scotland) Act 1995, Sched 3, para 2. Although this provision dates from the Criminal Procedure (Scotland) Act 1887, it was accepted at common law that an indictment did not have to state any *nomen juris*: See Hume, *Commentaries*, Vol ii, p 169; Alison, *Principles and Practice of the Criminal Law of Scotland*, Vol ii, p 230.
[5] The challenge is raised by means of a plea in bar of trial, known as a 'plea to the relevancy' of the indictment or complaint.

criminal according to the general principles of law recognised by civilised nations.'

The principle of legality is, however, additionally embodied in those Convention provisions which permit national authorities to take steps which interfere with individual rights, provided such interference is 'in accordance with [the] law'[6] or according to measures which are 'prescribed by law'.[7] It is also implicit in other references in the Convention to procedures or measures carried out in respect of the individual which must be done in a manner 'provided by law'.[8]

In applying Article 7, and other provisions which embody the principle of legality, the Strasbourg institutions have developed a number of general principles which may be summarised as follows:

(a) Retrospective application of the criminal law to the accused's disadvantage is prohibited.[9]

(b) Crimes and penalties must be defined by laws which are 'accessible' and 'foreseeable'.[10]

This need not be 'written law' in the sense of a code or other legislative text. In a common law system, rule of the common law may provide a sufficient basis for the criminal convictions referred to in Article 7.[11]

'Accessibility' means that an individual must have an indication of the legal rules applicable in a given case.[12] When referring to criminal legislation the Court has indicated that the requirement of 'accessibility' will be met if the law in question is 'published'.[13] It has not, however, indicated what requirements must be met with regard to accessibility of common law rules of criminal law.

So far as concerns the issue of 'foreseeability', the Court has indicated that absolute certainty in the criminal law is unattainable. A degree of flexibility is a necessary, indeed inevitable, aspect of the criminal law. However, the criminal law must be foreseeable with 'reasonable certainty'.[14] What this means is that the individual must be in a position to know from the terms of the law what acts and

---

[6] Art 8(2) (interference with privacy), Art 9(2).
[7] Art 5(1) (deprivation of liberty), Art 9(2) (interference with freedom of religion), Art 10(2) (interference with freedom of expression), Art 11(2) (interference with freedom of assembly and association).
[8] Art 2(1) (the death penalty).
[9] *Kokkinakis v Greece*, European Court of Human Rights, Series A, No 260–A. Retrospective application of a criminal law where this operates to the accused's advantage, as, for example, where by application of the *in mitius* principle on conviction a less severe penalty is applied to an offence than that which was applicable at the time the offence was committed. See, for example, *G v France*, European Court of Human Rights, 29/1994/47/6/557 (1995).
[10] *SW v United Kingdom*, European Court of Human Rights, Series A No 000, para 33. See also, *Kokkinakis v Greece*, European Court of Human Rights, Series A, No 260–A; *G v France*, European Court of Human Rights, 29/1994/476/557 (1995).
[11] *SW v United Kingdom*, Commission Opinion at para 46; *CR v United Kingdom*, Commission Opinion at para 47.
[12] *SW v United Kingdom*, Commission Opinion at para 44; *CR v United Kingdom*, Commission Opinion at para 45.
[13] See, for example, *Kopp v Switzerland* (1999) 27 EHRR 91; *Groppera Radio AG and Others v Switzerland* (1990) 13 EHRR 321.
[14] *SW v United Kingdom*, Commission Opinion at para 45; *Sunday Times v United Kingdom*, Series A, No 30, para 49; *CR v United Kingdom*, Commission Opinion at para 46.

omissions will make him criminally liable. In making this assessment it may be necessary to take into account the interpretation of the law by national courts.[15]

(c) The criminal law must not be extensively construed to an accused's detriment.

Judicial development of the criminal law is not prohibited. The Strasbourg institutions have recognised that an element of judicial interpretation is inevitable,[16] and in the United Kingdom (and, indeed, other Convention states) the 'progressive development' of the criminal law through judicial decisions is a 'well-entrenched and necessary part of legal tradition'.[17] Article 7 of the Convention cannot, therefore, be read as prohibiting 'the gradual clarification of the rules of criminal liability through judicial interpretation from case to case.'[18]

However, where the criminal law is developed 'by application and interpretation of courts in a common law system, their law-making function must remain within reasonable limits.'[19] Article 7(1) is intended to ensure that acts which were not previously punishable should not be held by the courts to involve criminal liability, and that existing offences should not be extended to cover facts which previously 'did not clearly constitute a criminal offence'.[20]

Article 7(1) does not prohibit the clarification of the existing elements of an offence, or their adaptation to new circumstances or developments in society.[21] However, the constituent elements of an offence may not be 'essentially changed to the detriment of an accused' and any 'progressive development by way of interpretation' must satisfy the test of reasonable foreseeability.[22] Judicial development of the criminal law is only permissible where such developments can reasonably be brought under the original concept of the offence,[23] or at least be 'consistent with the essence of the offence'.[24]

Flexibility and legality in Scots law

To what extent does Scots law comply with the requirements of the Convention? In order to answer this question it is necessary to compare contemporary Scottish practice with the principles established by the Court for the application of the principle of legality.

---

[15] *Kokkinakis v Greece*, European Court of Human Rights, Series A, No 260–A.
[16] *SW v United Kingdom*, Court at para 36; *CR v United Kingdom*, Court at para 34.
[17] Ibid.
[18] Ibid.
[19] *SW and CR v United Kingdom*, Commission Opinion, at paras 47 and 48.
[20] Application No 8710/79, DR 28, at p 77; *SW and CR v United Kingdom*, Commission Opinion at paras 47 and 48.
[21] Application 8710/79; 10505/83, DR 41, at p 178; Application 13079, DR 60, p 256; *SW and CR v United Kingdom*, Commission Opinion at paras 48 and 49.
[22] 8710/79; 10505/83; 13079; *SW and CR v United Kingdom*, Commission Opinion at paras 48 and 49.
[23] Ibid.
[24] *SW and CR v United Kingdom*, Court at paras 36/34.

(a) The rule against retrospective criminal law: the 'declaratory power'

No clearer example of a conflict with this aspect of the principle of legality could be found than the so-called 'declaratory power' of the High Court of Justiciary. This power was expressly recognised for the first time in Baron Hume's *Commentaries on the Law of Scotland Respecting the Description and Punishment of Crimes*, published in 1797.[25] In the Introduction to this work, Hume pointed out various ways in which Scottish criminal practice demonstrated advantages over the criminal law of England. In doing so he stated:

> 'Another point in which the custom of the two countries remarkably differs, is with respect to the punishment of new crimes or modes of transgression. It seems to be held in England, that no Court has the power to take cognisance of any new offence, although highly pernicious, and approaching very nearly to others which had been prohibited, until some statute has declared it to be a crime, and assigned a punishment. With us the maxim is directly the reverse: that our Supreme Court have an inherent power as such competently to punish (with the exception of life and limb) every act which is obviously of a criminal nature; though it be such which in time past has never been the subject of prosecution.'

Even for its time this was a fairly remarkable claim, and Hume offers surprisingly little authority to support it. Indeed, Hume refers to only two suggested examples of the exercise of this power, neither of which, in fact, support Hume's assertion of a judicial power to create new crimes.[26]

In practice, the courts have been reluctant to rely upon this power to create new crimes, at least overtly. There is, in fact, only one reported instance of the court openly relying upon the declaratory power and that is the case of *Bernard Greenhuff*.[27] In that case, a full bench of the High Court endorsed Hume's

---

[25] The fourth edition of this work, published in 1844, is today the standard reference edition, and hereafter referred to as: Hume, *Commentaries*. This work is today regarded as enjoying 'Institutional' status, in relation to the criminal law in the sense that, in the absence of a relevant precedent or statutory provision, the views of Hume (like other so-called 'institutional writers') may be relied upon by the courts as determinative of the criminal law.

[26] The first of these—the sending of 'incendiary or threatening letters'—appears to be a reference to the case of *John Gray*, decided in 1737 Hume, i, 441). However, as Lord Cockburn pointed out in the case of *Bernard Greenhuff* (1838) 2 Swinton 236, there was no need in that case for reliance upon any such power, since *John Gray* was in fact a case of extortion, and there was nothing novel about the case other than the means adopted by the accused to make his demands. The second example, the 'corruption or alteration of bills, promissory-notes and the like to the prejudice of the acceptor', is so vague as to be unidentifiable, but in any case would seem to be a not very surprising example of the crime of falsehood, fraud and wilful imposition. Hume's understanding of the law is supported by Alison, *Principles of the Criminal Law of Scotland* (1832) p 624, but all of his examples refer to cases decided after Hume asserted the existence of the declaratory power, and some are not examples of the court declaring new crimes at all.

[27] (1838) 2 Swinton 236. The existence of a declaratory power seems to have been accepted by a majority of the court in *Taylor and Others*, 19 October 1808, Burnett, *A Treatise on Various Branches of the Criminal Law of Scotland*, 1811, Appendix X. The case concerned an alleged criminal combination by workers in the paper industry to raise wages. A majority of the court held that the indictment did not disclose an offence—even allowing for the possibility of the court declaring such a combination to be criminal.

statement of the law, and held that it had the power to declare criminal the 'opening and keeping a common gaming-house for the playing of games of chance for money, for the profit of the keepers, and where games of chance are commonly and publicly played for money'.[28] There was only one dissent. Lord Cockburn was adamant that the court had no such power to create a 'totally original offence',[29] and that such a power was 'inconsistent with the proper constitutional limits of any British court'.[30] As we will see, however, while rejecting the declaratory power, Lord Cockburn left open to future generations of judges and prosecutors an alternative technique for judicial development of the law which, since it avoids open acceptance of a power of judicial legislation, has proved to be a far more fruitful source of new crimes than the declaratory power in its fullest sense.

Although the declaratory power has not been explicitly applied by the court since *Bernard Greenhuff*, it is possible to point to several cases in which it has been used to extend the criminal law in quite novel directions.

Perhaps the clearest example of the unacknowledged use of the declaratory power is to be found in the case of *Strathern v Seaforth* in 1925.[31] In this case, the accused was charged with 'clandestinely' taking possession of a motor car, and driving it in various streets in Glasgow, knowing that he had not received permission from the owner to do so, and knowing that he would not have received such permission.

An objection was taken to the charge on the ground that it did not disclose a crime known to the law of Scotland. This was sustained by the sheriff, but the High Court upheld an appeal by the Crown against this decision. Although counsel for the respondent appears to have argued that the court was being asked to declare for the first time that 'the *furtum usus* of the Roman law was a crime according to the law of Scotland'[32] none of the judges in the High Court referred to the declaratory power. Nevertheless, while the Lord Justice-Clerk (Alness) thought that the Crown's contention (that this was a crime) was supported by the authorities cited to the court, he felt able to state that he would 'not have required any authority to convince [him] that the circumstances set out in this complaint are sufficient, if unexplained, and proved, to constitute an offence against the law of Scotland.'[33] In other words, his Lordship would have been able to identify for himself and uphold the criminality of the accused's conduct without reference to any relevant precedent.

More recent cases suggest that while, in principle, the declaratory power remains available to prosecutors and the courts, in practice it is not relied upon. It appears that the Lord Advocate was prepared to ask the court to exercise the power in the case of *Khaliq v H M Advocate*[34] although, in the event, it proved

---

[28] Ibid at 237.
[29] Ibid at 274.
[30] Ibid at 274–275.
[31] 1926 JC 100 1926 SLT 445. That this case involved an exercise of the declaratory power is supported by an observation by the Lord Justice-Clerk (Aitchison) in *Sugden v H M Advocate* 1934 JC 103 at 109, where his Lordship described *Strathern v Seaforth* as a modern example of the exercise of the declaratory power. For a further example of unacknowledged use of the declaratory power, see *Kerr v Hill* 1936 JC 71, 1936 SLT 320.
[32] 1926 SLT 445 at 445.
[33] Ibid.
[34] 1984 JC 23, 1984 SLT 137, 1983 SCCR 483.

unnecessary for the prosecutor to do so. In *Grant* v *Allan*[35] the prosecutor did in fact propose to the court that it should, if necessary, rely upon the declaratory power to declare criminal the dishonest appropriation of commercially valuable confidential information. Having examined the authorities, the Lord Justice-Clerk (Ross) concluded that the complaint did not disclose a crime, and turned to the question of the declaratory power. Lord Ross then stated[36]:

> 'Although there are circumstances where it will be appropriate for the court to exercise this power, I am of opinion that great care must be taken in the exercise of this power. Exercising the power may well conflict with the principle *nullum crimen sine lege*. The declaratory power has been considered in a number of cases of the last 50 years. I do not find it necessary to consider these cases because I am not satisfied that what is libelled in this complaint was so obviously of a criminal nature that it should be treated as a crime under the criminal law. No doubt what the appellant is alleged to have done was reprehensible and immoral, but . . . the fact that conduct is reprehensible or indicates moral delinquency is not sufficient to bring it within the scope of the criminal law. I recognise that there may be reasons for thinking that conduct of this kind ought to be regarded as criminal. However, if that is so, I am of opinion that it is for Parliament and not the courts to create any new crime in that regard.'

The declaratory power's origins are dubious. Its exercise has been fitful, and although it has been used on occasion without acknowledgement, it has not been openly relied on for over 150 years. There can be little doubt that any attempt to use it in the future would be incompatible with Article 7(1) of the Convention. The only possible question which does arise is whether the exercise of the declaratory power in this sense could be rescued by an appeal to Article 7(2). This envisages the creation of an offence in relation to conduct which is not already criminal according to the law of Scotland, but which was, at the time the accused engaged in that conduct, 'criminal according to the general principles of law recognised by civilised nations'. It has generally been understood that Article 7(2) is intended to permit states to impose punishment under domestic law for violations of internationally recognised standards (for example, by permitting a state to apply, retrospectively, domestic laws to crimes against humanity or violations of the laws and customs of war). It has been argued, however, that it is not so limited, and could be invoked, more generally, to permit the retrospective application of domestic criminal law to 'cover other offences involving fundamentally immoral conduct that is generally regarded as criminal in national law.'[37] Leaving aside the point that to interpret Article 7(2) in such a broad manner would tend to fundamentally undermine the protective effect of Article 7(1), it is difficult to see how it can be invoked to rescue the application of the criminal law in those cases where it has been openly applied—as in *Greenhuff*, or more covertly applied, as in

---

[35] 1987 JC 71, 1988 SLT 11, 1987 SCCR 402.
[36] 1988 SLT 11 at 14.
[37] See D J Harris, M O'Boyle and C Warbrick, *Law of the European Convention on Human Rights* (1995) p 282. See also, S Styles, 'Something to Declare: A Defence of the Declaratory Power of the High Court of Justiciary' in R F Hunter (ed), *Justice and Crime* (1993) pp 211–231 at p 224.

Strathern v *Seaforth*. It would certainly be difficult to argue that running a public gaming-house, vehicular joy-riding or making a false report to the police[38] were examples of conduct which was criminal 'according to the general principles of law recognised by civilised nations'. At the very least, any attempt to invoke the declaratory power would put the Crown to the task of demonstrating that the conduct, not hitherto visited by criminal sanctions in Scotland, satisfied this requirement. Given the already expansive nature of Scottish criminal law, it is submitted that this would be somewhat difficult.

(b) Criminal laws must be accessible and foreseeable

As we have seen, the Convention requires that rules of the criminal law be accessible and foreseeable, so that the individual may, with 'reasonable certainty', know what acts and omissions will make him criminally liable. Crimes which are too broad, or which are stated in vague and uncertain terms are, therefore, incompatible with the Convention.

While most offences do, of course, meet the standards required by the Convention, there are important examples of offences which appear to reject the need for precise definition. The two most notorious examples are the crimes of shameless indecency and breach of the peace in which reasonable certainty has been abandoned in favour of a catch-all approach.

This can be seen first of all in an open judicial acceptance of the absence of precise limits to these offences. The *locus classicus* of this attitude is to be found in the opinion of the Lord Justice-General (Clyde) in the case of *McLaughlan* v *Boyd*.[39] In that case the accused was charged with using 'lewd, indecent and libidinous practices' towards a number of adult persons. He was convicted, and appealed on the ground that 'lewd, indecent and libidinous practices' were only criminal if used towards persons below the age of puberty. In refusing the appeal, and upholding the general proposition that 'all shamelessly indecent conduct is criminal', the Lord Justice-General (Clyde) observed: 'It would be a mistake to imagine that the criminal common law of Scotland countenances any precise and exact categorisation of the forms of conduct which amount to crime. It has been pointed out many times in this Court that such is not the nature or quality of the criminal law of Scotland.'[40]

This attitude is reflected in the opinion of Lord Cameron in the case of *Watt* v *Annan*,[41] another case of shameless indecency. According to his Lordship:

> 'It would be impracticable as well as undesirable to attempt to define precisely the limits and ambit of this particular offence ... If it were considered desirable or necessary that this was a chapter of the criminal law in which precise boundaries or limits were to be set then it might be thought that the task is one which is more appropriate for the hand of the legislator.'[42]

In similar vein the 'open texture' of breach of the peace has been freely

---

[38] See *Kerr* v *Hill* 1936 JC 71, 1936 SLT 320.
[39] 1934 JC 19, 1933 SLT 629.
[40] 1933 SLT 629 at 631.
[41] 1978 JC 84, 1978 SLT 198.
[42] 1978 SLT 198 at 201.

acknowledged by the High Court. In *Young* v *Heatly*[43] Lord Justice-General (Clyde) observed that: 'Breach of the peace . . . is an offence the limits of which have never been sharply defined. It is so largely in each case a question of circumstance and of degree.'

The offence requires proof of an actual disturbance of the peace or, in the absence of such proof, 'something . . . done in breach of public order or decorum which might reasonably be expected to lead to the lieges[44] being alarmed or upset.'[45] The test is an objective one, so that mere evidence of alarm on the part of an individual will not necessarily lead to the conclusion that there has been a breach of the peace.[46]

In *Montgomery* v *McLeod*[47] the High Court freely acknowledged the open-ended nature of this offence, stating that: '[t]here is no limit to the kind of conduct which may give rise to a charge of breach of the peace'[48] provided that the conduct was such as to fall within the above definition.

The breadth of these offences only really becomes apparent when one considers the vast variety of circumstances to which they have been applied. Breach of the peace has been held to include such diversely anti-social behaviour as: 'peeping' into houses at night[49]; causing embarrassment by making indecent remarks to adult women in an hotel bar[50]; playing marbles in the street on a Sunday afternoon[51]; threatening to commit suicide in a public place[52]; cross-dressing in the red-light area of Aberdeen[53]; begging[54]; sitting on a felled tree as a protest at its destruction and obstructing its being cut up[55]; loitering in and about a liquor store in a suspicious manner[56]; playing football in the street at night[57]; injecting oneself in a locked toilet cubicle[58]; alarming a third party by glue-sniffing in their presence[59]; shouting political slogans (in support, *inter alia*, of the IRA) outside a football ground[60]; distributing pamphlets seeking support for pupil power and sexual freedom to

---

[43] 1959 JC 66, 1959 SLT 250.
[44] Ie the public.
[45] *Raffaeli* v *Heatly* 1949 JC 101; 1949 SLT 284; *Young* v *Heatly* 1959 JC 66, 1959 SLT 250. *Cf. Donaldson* v *Vannet* 1998 SLT 957, 1998 SCCR 421.
[46] *Donaldson* v *Vannet* 1998 SCCR 421.
[47] 1977 SLT(N) 77, (1977) SCCR Supplement 164.
[48] 1997 SLT(N) 77 at 78.
[49] *Raffaeli* v *Heatly* 1949 JC 101; 1949 SLT 284. See also *McDougall* v *Dochree* 1992 JC 154, 1992 SLT 624, 1992 SCCR 531—watching women using a sunbed by peeping through a hole in a partition separating a toilet cubicle and the solarium where the sunbed was located.
[50] *Sinclair* v *Annan* 1980 SLT (Notes) 55.
[51] *John Meekison and Tutor* v *Mackay* (1848) Arkley 503.
[52] *John MacLean, The Scotsman*, 30 October 1979 (Inverness Sheriff Court).
[53] *Stewart* v *Lockhart* 1990 SCCR 390.
[54] *Wyness* v *Lockhart* 1992 SCCR 808. But see also *Donaldson* v *Vannet*, above, note 46, which holds that begging *per se* cannot be regarded as breach of the peace—although begging in a manner likely to cause alarm may do so.
[55] *Colhoun* v *Friel* 1996 SLT 1252, 1996 SCCR 497.
[56] *McKenzie* v *Normand* 1992 SLT 130, 1992 SCCR 14.
[57] *Cameron* v *Normand* 1992 SCCR 866.
[58] *Thompson* v *MacPhail* 1989 SLT 637, 1989 SCCR 266. In this case, the court held that the facts proved did not amount to a breach of the peace, while at the same time confirming that such conduct could, in appropriate circumstances, do so.
[59] *Taylor* v *Hamilton* 1984 SCCR 393. In the earlier case of *Fisher* v *Keane* 1981 JC 50 1981 SLT (Notes) 28 it had been held that glue-sniffing was not, *per se*, a breach of the peace.
[60] *Duffield* v *Skeen* 1981 SCCR 66.

young girls to the annoyance of their parents[61]; and repeatedly executing handbrake turns and causing a car to skid in a public car park.[62]

The crime of conducting oneself in a 'shamelessly indecent manner' has been held to include conduct akin to indecent assault[63]; showing an obscene film in private to an audience of adults[64]; quasi-incestuous conduct between a man and his 16-year-old daughter[65]; sexual relations between a man and his foster daughter[66]; selling, exposing for sale and keeping for sale indecent magazines, books and sex gadgets[67]; showing an obscene video-recording to two teenage girls in private[68]; and presenting (although apparently not performing) an indecent display in a public house.[69] In *Dean v John Menzies (Holdings) Ltd*,[70] a company incorporated under the Companies Acts was charged with conducting itself in a shamelessly indecent manner by selling and exposing for sale in its shops allegedly indecent and obscene magazines. The High Court, sensing perhaps that things had gone too far, concluded that while a company could perhaps be guilty of a common law offence requiring proof of *mens rea*, it would not be appropriate to hold that a company could conduct itself in a shamelessly indecent manner.

It is difficult to argue that offences which are capable of such elasticity satisfy standards of foreseeability and certainty. The European Court of Human Rights has held that the English concept of breach of the peace is not so uncertain as to fall foul of the Convention.[71] While there may be some uncertainty about the definition of breach of the peace in English law, there is no evidence to suggest that the English courts are prepared to apply that concept to such a broad range of offending behaviour as the Scottish courts have done.

Examples may also be found of the courts basing their decisions on rules which, it is suggested, hardly satisfy the requirement of accessibility. The case of *Khaliq* v *H M Advocate*[72] is just such a case. In this case, the appellants were charged with 'culpably, wilfully and recklessly' supplying glue-sniffing kits to a large number of children aged from eight to fifteen years, knowing that the children intended to use these kits for the purpose of inhalation of the solvent vapours, and knowing that such inhalation was, or could be, dangerous to the lives or health of the children, and that the consequence of their actions was to cause or procure the inhalation of the vapours by the children to the danger of their health and lives. An objection to the relevancy of the indictment on the ground that it did not disclose a crime was rejected by the trial judge and the accused appealed.

On appeal it was held that the indictment was relevant. The Crown's argument

---

[61] *Turner v Kennedy* (1972) SCCR Supplement 30.
[62] *Horsburgh v Russell* 1994 SLT 942, 1994 SCCR 237.
[63] *McLaughlan v Boyd*, above.
[64] *Watt v Annan* 1978 SLT 198.
[65] *R v H M Advocate* 1988 SLT 623, 1988 SCCR 254.
[66] *H M Advocate v K* 1994 SCCR 499. In this case, the accused was a married man. However, it is worth noting that the effect of the decision is to criminalise sexual relations between two persons who, had they both been unmarried, would have been free to marry.
[67] *Robertson v Smith* 1980 JC 1, 1979 SLT (Notes) 51; *Scott v Smith* 1981 JC 46, 1981 SLT (Notes) 22 *Ingram v Macari* 1983 SLT 61, 1982 SCCR 372; *Tudhope v Barlow* 1981 SLT (Sh Ct) 94.
[68] *Carmichael v Ashrif* 1985 SCCR 461.
[69] *Lockhart v Stephen* 1987 SCCR 642 (Sh Ct).
[70] 1981 JC 23, 1981 SLT 50.
[71] *Steel and Others v United Kingdom*.
[72] See note 34 above.

was that what was charged here was 'not a new crime, but merely a modern example of conduct which our law has for long regarded as criminal'. The Crown relied on the following passage from Hume[73]:

> 'Let us now attend to those offences against the person, which remain on the footing of the common law, and are punishable only with some inferior pain, at the discretion of the Court. These are various in kind and degree; and the law is provided with sundry corresponding terms for them, more or less comprehensive, and commonly employed in libels, such as assault, invasion, beating and bruising, blooding and wounding, stabbing, mutilation, demembration, and some others. But although the injury do not come under any of the terms of style, nor be such as can be announced in a single phrase, this circumstance in nowise affects the competency of a prosecution. Let the libel, in the *major* proposition, give an intelligible account of it in terms at large; and, if it amounts to a real injury, it shall be sustained to infer punishment, less or more, *pro modo admisso*; no matter how new or strange the wrong.'

This passage was relied upon by the Lord Justice-General (Emslie) in reaching the conclusion that the indictment was relevant. In his view, the passage referred to provided a 'general principle' under which the appellant's conduct could be brought so as to make it the subject of a criminal charge. That 'principle' was that 'within the category of conduct identified as criminal are acts, whatever their nature may be, which cause real injury to the person.'[74]

Taken literally, and without reference to context, that appears to be what Hume says. Let us, however, look at the context: Hume's discussion of these common law crimes comes after a discussion of various named, statutory offences, most of them capital, of violence against the person.[75] The point Hume is making is not that all examples of 'real injury' are crimes. What he is saying is that all examples of *personal violence* are criminal, even though they cannot be brought within the scope of recognised, existing labels. Indeed, with the sole exception of the cursing of parents, which was a statutory crime, there is no offence, and no example of an offence, discussed in Hume's chapter 'Of Real Injuries' which does not involve personal violence, or at least an assault which threatens personal violence. A discussion which ranges over mutilation, biting off noses, assault with intent to ravish, stabbing, blinding and branding, in a textbook first published in the late 18th century, is hardly an 'accessible' source of legal rules.

(c) Judicial development of the law must be confined within reasonable limits

The principle of legality is intended to restrain the unreasonable or unpredictable extension of recognised criminal laws. In terms of statutory crimes, the principle often finds its expression in the rule of strict construction of penal statutes, a rule

---

[73] 3rd edn, Vol i, 327; 2nd edn, Vol i, 322; 4th edn, Vol i, 327.
[74] 1984 SLT 137 at 143.
[75] The only clear exception being the statutory crime of cursing of parents under the statute 1661, cap 20.

which, somewhat paradoxically, is accepted and applied by the Scottish courts.[76] The matter is, however, quite otherwise in relation to the common law, and numerous examples of frequently dramatic extensions of common law crimes can be pointed to. In all of these cases, although the court has purported merely to be applying existing crimes, they have in reality, created new criminal offences.

A particularly striking example of this is to be found in the case of *H M Advocate* v *Wilson*.[77] In that case, the respondent was charged with the common law crime of malicious mischief. The indictment narrated that he had 'wilfully, recklessly and maliciously' activated an emergency stop button in one of the turbine halls of Hunterston Power Station, thereby bringing to a halt one of the turbines in the power station, thus causing a loss of generation of over 12 million kilowatt hour units of electricity, which had to be replaced and fed into the national grid from other sources, at a cost of £147,000.

The accused objected to the indictment on the ground that, since the Crown conceded that it contained a charge of malicious mischief, and since malicious mischief required proof of physical damage to corporeal property, and since there was no allegation of any such damage, it was irrelevant. This objection was upheld by the sheriff, but repelled by the High Court on appeal. Again, the High Court resorted to Hume, and were able to find in Hume's discussion of the crime of malicious mischief support for the view that this crime may be committed even without actual damage to property if there is 'interference' with property which causes 'patrimonial loss' to the victim.

What might be described as the 'technical' objections to this conclusion are too detailed to be pursued here.[78] Suffice it to say that the court is only able to reach this conclusion by ignoring the context in which Hume uses such phrases, and in particular by failing to note that there is no instance of malicious damage discussed by Hume (or anyone else for that matter) which does not involve physical damage to, or destruction of, corporeal property. The decision is a very clear example of an unwarranted extension of an existing offence, whose definition, or at least the relevant element of that definition, had been settled for more than 200 years.[79]

PROSECUTORIAL DISCRETION

The Lord Advocate, and those acting on his behalf as prosecutors, enjoy a degree of discretion in relation to the prosecution of crime which is probably unique in the English-speaking world, and which is unparalleled in any other European Union country.

The fundamental principle which governs the prosecution of crime in Scotland is that the Lord Advocate is 'the master of the instance in all prosecutions in the

---

[76] *Mackenzie* v *H M Advocate* 1969 JC 52, 1970 SLT 81; *Friel* v *Initial Contract Services Ltd* 1994 SLT 1216, 1993 SCCR 675; *Barty* v *Hill* 1907 SC (J) 36, (1907) 14 SLT 616.
[77] 1984 SLT 117, 1983 SCCR 420.
[78] But see Gane and Stoddart, *Casebook on Scottish Criminal Law* (2nd edn, pp 633–638).
[79] *Cf. Bett* v *Hamilton* 1997 SLT 1310, 1997 SCCR 621. A similar approach can be found in many other areas of the criminal law. See, for examples, *H M Advocate* v *Martin and Others* 1956 JC 1, 1956 SLT 193, where the crime of hindering or frustrating the ends of justice was extended to escaping from prison while working outside the prison.

public interest.'[80] In *Boyle v H M Advocate*[81] Lord Cameron summed up the content of this principle in the following terms:

> 'In Scotland the master of the instance in all prosecutions for the public interest is the Lord Advocate. It is for him to decide when and against whom to launch prosecution and upon what charges. It is for him to decide in which court they shall be prosecuted. It is for him to decide what pleas of guilt he will accept and it is for him to decide when to withdraw or abandon proceedings. Not only so, even when a verdict of guilt has been returned and recorded it still lies with the Lord Advocate whether to move the court to pronounce sentence and without that motion no sentence can be pronounced or imposed.'[82]

This is quite an astonishing breadth of discretion. It arises, in part, because of the special position which the office of Lord Advocate has come to occupy in the Scottish firmament, and, in part, because of other features of the Scottish system of criminal justice which are logically unconnected, but which, in practice, have a close relationship to the position of the Lord Advocate.

Notable amongst these is the absence of any formal classification of crimes by reference to which the mode or venue of a criminal trial is determined. English law once drew a distinction between felonies and misdemeanours (as most American states continue to do) but now has a three-fold classification of offences: indictable, summary and offences triable either way. French law has its classification into *crimes*, *délits* and *contraventions*; Spanish law distinguishes between *delitos* and *faltas*; and such classifications are to be found throughout Europe. Apart from the attribution of offences such as murder and rape to the exclusive jurisdiction of the High Court, or the legislative allocation of some statutory offences to summary jurisdiction, or to the High Court, Scots law contains virtually no mandatory rules on the court in which a given offence is to be tried, or the form of procedure to be followed. This would be regarded by many European lawyers as extraordinary enough, but when one adds to it the consideration that one of the parties to the case is entitled to determine the venue, this would be regarded as even more surprising, and in some systems unconstitutional.

Nor is the public prosecutor in Scotland troubled by such considerations as the so-called *legaliteitsprinzip* or *principe de la légalité des poursuites*. According to this principle, the state, when presented with sufficient evidence of a crime, is required to prosecute. This principle may be avoided in a variety of ways, and even in systems (such as the German) where the principle is said to apply it is not punctiliously observed. In many systems, however, it remains the case that the public prosecutor is not free to refuse to prosecute, or to abandon proceedings, based upon his or her assessment of the demands of public interest.

---

[80] *Boyle v H M Advocate* 1976 JC 32, 1976 SLT 126.
[81] Above.
[82] 1976 SLT 126 at 126.

Challenging prosecutorial discretion: the common law

Not only does the public prosecutor enjoy extensive discretion in relation to the prosecution of crime, but the extent to which that discretion is subject to review is, in practice, quite limited.

(a) Challenging the decision to prosecute

The decision to prosecute may be challenged on the ground that, in proceeding, the prosecutor is acting oppressively. The plea of oppression may be raised as a plea in bar of trial on the ground of prejudicial pre-trial publicity,[83] delay in bringing the case to court,[84] and in certain other cases[85] where there is a threat to the accused's right to a fair trial which is so grave that it could not be removed by an appropriate direction to the jury or the trial court.[86] In practice, it is not easy to satisfy this test, and the occasions on which pleas in bar of trial are upheld on the ground of oppression are uncommon.

There are suggestions that the court has the power to stay criminal proceedings where, in the light of the conduct of the prosecuting authorities, it would be an abuse of the process of the court to allow the case to proceed.[87] However, the correctness of these as a general statement of Scots law is open to doubt, and it has been suggested that the doctrine may only apply in cases which have an 'international' dimension.[88]

It is not open to uphold a plea of oppression on the ground that the prosecution is ill-advised, or that the prosecutor has acted unfairly or in some other way of which the court might disapprove, if the accused's right to a fair trial is not prejudiced.[89]

(b) Challenging the decision not to prosecute

The possibilities for mounting a challenge to a decision *not* to prosecute are, if anything, even more limited. The only means whereby a decision not to prosecute can be challenged, is by private prosecution. This is a rare event: only two successful private prosecutions in solemn proceedings have been brought this century.[90] A person wishing to bring a private prosecution must show that he or she has a special interest in the prosecution of the offence, over and above that which is shared by the general public, and it would seem that a private

---

[83] *Stuurman* v *H M Advocate* 1980 JC 111, 1980 SLT (Notes) 95; *Donnelly* v *H M Advocate* 1984 SCCR 93; *X* v *Sweeney* 1982 JC 70, 1983 SLT 48, 1982 SCCR 161.
[84] *McFadyen* v *Annan* 1992 JC 53, 1992 SLT 163, 1992 SCCR 186.
[85] See, for example, *Mowbray* v *Crowe* 1993 JC 212, 1994 SLT 445, 1993 SCCR 730; *Bott* v *Anderson* 1995 JC 178, 1995 SLT 1308, 1995 SCCR 584.
[86] See, generally, G H Gordon, *Renton and Brown's Criminal Procedure* (6th edn, 1996) para 9.21 *et seq*.
[87] *Bennett, Petitioner* 1995 SLT 510, 1994 SCCR 902.
[88] See *Torres* v *H M Advocate* 1997 SCCR 491.
[89] See, for example, *H M Advocate* v *Boyle* 1993 JC 5, 1993 SLT 1079, 1992 SCCR 939; *H M Advocate* v *O'Neill* 1992 SLT 303, 1992 SCCR 130; *Hamilton* v *Byrne* 1997 SLT 1210, 1997 SCCR 547; *Latto* v *Vannet* 1997 SCCR 721.
[90] *J & P Coats Ltd* v *Brown* 1909 SC(J) 29, (1909) 6 Adam 19; *X* v *Sweeney* note 84 above.

prosecution for certain offences of a 'public' nature (such as perjury and other offences affecting the administration of justice) will be permitted only in the most exceptional circumstances.[91]

The very limited means available for challenging prosecutorial decisions means that, in practice, the exercise of prosecutorial discretion in Scotland is subject to very little external control.[92] In particular, it appears that the decisions of the public prosecutor are not subject to judicial review.[93] It is true that this matter has not been tested before the courts, but the Court of Session (which has exclusive jurisdiction in matters of judicial review) has stated that it has no competence to pronounce in matters of prosecutorial discretion.[94]

Convention rights and challenges to prosecutorial discretion

The Human Rights Act and the Scotland Act both raise the possibility of a challenge to prosecutorial discretion on the ground that it has been exercised in a manner which is incompatible with Convention rights.

(a) Review under the Human Rights Act

The Human Rights Act clearly contemplates review of prosecutorial decisions on the ground of incompatibility with Convention rights. It is clear that the public prosecutor is a 'public authority' for the purpose of section 6 of the Human Rights Act, so that it will be unlawful under section 6(1) of that Act for the prosecutor to act in a manner which is incompatible with a Convention right. A person who claims that a public authority has acted, or proposes to act, in a way which is unlawful under section 6 may bring proceedings against the authority, or rely on the Convention right or rights concerned in any legal proceedings at the instance of the public authority, provided that he or she is, or would be, a 'victim' of the unlawful act.[95] So, provided that a decision to prosecute (or not to do so) is incompatible with a Convention right, it is subject to review on that ground, whether by judicial review, or by way of defence to criminal proceedings or, presumably, as an argument in support of an application to bring a private prosecution.

---

[91] See, generally, *J & P Coats Ltd v Brown*, above; *X v Sweeney*, above; *McBain v Crichton* 1961 JC 25, 1961 SLT 209; *Trapp v M, Trapp v Y* 1971 SLT (Notes) 30; *Meehan v Inglis* 1975 JC 9, 1974 SLT (Notes) 61.
[92] It is, however, subject to the internal controls and guidance of the prosecution service itself, but these guidelines are confidential and not normally available to anyone outside the service. See S Moody and J Tombs, *Prosecution in the Public Interest* (1982) at p 20.
[93] Duff describes this as 'the conventional view' and suggests that this remedy might be available on ordinary administrative law grounds. See P Duff, 'The Prosecution Service; Independence and Accountability' in P Duff and N Hutton (eds), *Criminal Justice in Scotland* (1999) pp 115–130 at p 128.
[94] See *Law Hospital N.H.S. Trust v Lord Advocate* 1996 sc 301, 1996 SLT 848. The courts in England have held that decisions to prosecute and not to prosecute are subject to judicial review. See *R v Inland Revenue Commissioners, ex parte Mead* [1993] 1 All ER 772; *R v General Council of the Bar, ex parte Percival* [1991] 1 QB 212, [1990] 3 WLR 323, [1990] 3 All ER 137. See, generally, J Fionda, *Public Prosecutors and Discretion: A Comparative Study* (1995) Chapter 2.
[95] Human Rights Act, s 7(7).

(b) Review under the Scotland Act

Section 44 of the Scotland Act provides for the creation of a Scottish Executive, which includes the Lord Advocate and the Solicitor General for Scotland. Section 57(2) of the Act provides that a member of the Scottish Executive has no power to make any subordinate legislation, or to do any other act, so far as the legislation or act is incompatible with any of the Convention rights. This means, then, that prosecutorial decisions may be challenged under the Scotland Act on the ground that they are incompatible with Convention rights. For the purpose of the Scotland Act, such a question is a 'devolution issue' and therefore subject to the special procedures laid down in Schedule 6 to the Act.

(c) The decision to prosecute and Convention rights

The question which immediately rises, then, is when would a decision to prosecute, or not to prosecute, amount to a violation of a Convention right?

With respect to prosecution in violation of a Convention right, it is possible to identify two different types of case. The first is where the very fact of prosecution violates a Convention right. It is likely that challenges of this kind will be difficult to mount. One category of cases in which this kind of submission may arise will be those in which the prosecution is brought in violation of the principle of legality, as that forms part of the Convention rights.

The suggestion was raised in the cases of *T* v *United Kingdom* and *V* v *United Kingdom*[96] that the very fact of *prosecuting* two child defendants was inhumane and degrading. That suggestion has been rejected by the Court, and that is probably correct. However, the decision in that case raises a further question: if the only manner in which the accused could be *prosecuted* was under a procedure which *by its nature* involved a violation of a Convention right (in the instant case the right to a fair trial under Article 6(1)) could the prosecution be challenged? It is at least arguable that this would be a case in which the public authority (the prosecutor) 'proposes to act' in a way which is incompatible with a Convention right. If so, it is submitted that the proposed action could be challenged under section 7(1) of the Human Rights Act, and under section 57(2) of the Scotland Act.

A second, and much more common, type of case will be where the accused raises as a defence to a criminal prosecution the claim that the conduct alleged to be an offence is protected by a Convention right. So, for example, one might expect cases in which an accused charged with shameless indecency claims that the conduct is protected by the right to privacy under Article 8, where a demonstrator charged with breach of the peace claims that her conduct is protected by freedom of assembly under Article 11, or freedom of expression under Article 10.

In these cases, it may not be necessary for a prosecution to have been launched for Convention rights to become relevant. The lessons learned from cases such as *Dudgeon* v *United Kingdom*[97] and *Norris* v *Ireland*[98] are that persons who are 'at risk'

---

[96] European Court of Human Rights, 16 December 1999, [2000] 2 All ER 1024 (Note); 7 BHRC 659; 2000 Crim LR 187.
[97] (1981) 4 EHRR 149.
[98] (1998) 13 EHRR 186.

of a violation of their rights are entitled to claim to be victims of a violation of those rights without waiting until the measures are actually applied to them in violation of their rights. It is in this respect that the Act may bring about the most fundamental changes.

As the law presently stands, an individual who is under investigation for an alleged offence, or who has been charged with an offence, has no effective means of challenging these procedures at an early stage. This may, of course, be very important, particularly if the prosecution results in an acquittal. Section 7 of the Human Rights Act makes it clear that Convention rights can be invoked not only where the public authority has acted in a way which is incompatible with a Convention right, but also where the public authority 'proposes to act' in such a way. This raises, immediately, the possibility of a much earlier challenge to the prosecutor. Much, of course, depends upon what is embraced in the phrase 'proposes to act' but presumably, at the latest, service of a complaint or indictment indicates that the prosecutor 'proposes to act', and if that proposed action is incompatible with a Convention right then the 'victim' is entitled forthwith to challenge it on that ground. Could this happen at an earlier point in the proceedings—appearance on petition or judicial examination?

(d) Failure or refusal to prosecute as a violation of Convention rights

It was noted earlier that whereas there are various ways to challenge the launching of a prosecution, under our present arrangements the only legal challenge which can be brought against a decision not to prosecute is by means of an application to the High Court to bring a private prosecution. How will Convention rights affect the case where a decision has been taken not to proceed?

In order to answer that question it is important to note the extent to which a failure to prosecute might constitute a violation of Convention rights. The Convention does not guarantee to the victims of an alleged crime the right to have criminal proceedings instituted against a third party.[99] Nevertheless, it is clear that certain Articles of the Convention may impose upon the state the obligation to take positive steps to protect human rights, which may include an obligation to investigate alleged criminal offences and, where appropriate, bring proceedings with a view to punishing the offender. So, for example, in *X and Y v Netherlands*[100] it was held that the respondent state had violated the first applicant's right to privacy by failing to ensure that appropriate criminal sanctions were available to punish a man who had sexually abused her. In *Osman v United Kingdom*,[101] the Court ruled that Article 2 of the Convention did not merely impose upon the state an obligation to refrain from the unlawful and intentional taking of life. It also required the state to take appropriate steps to safeguard the lives of those within its jurisdiction, including, as necessary, effective criminal law provisions to deter the commission of offences against the person, backed up by effective law-enforcement mechanisms for the prevention, suppression and punishment of breaches of the criminal law.

---

[99] *Dubowska and Skup v Poland*, European Commission on Human Rights.
[100] 26 March 1985, Ser A No 91.
[101] (2000) 29 EHRR 245.

In certain cases, therefore, it may well be the case that a decision not to bring criminal proceedings will be incompatible with Convention rights, and therefore subject to challenge on that ground.

(e) Defences to Convention rights challenges

Section 6(2) of the Human Rights Act provides that it will not be unlawful for a public authority to act in a way which is incompatible with a Convention right if either of the following conditions applies:

> 'if (a)—as the result of one or more provisions of primary legislation, the authority could not have acted differently; or
>
> (b) in the case of one or more provisions of, or made under, primary legislation which cannot be read or given effect in a way which is compatible with the Convention rights, the authority was acting so as to give effect to or enforce those provisions.'

These provisions have particular relevance to the position of the public prosecutor in Scotland because of section 57(3) of the Scotland Act. As we have noted, section 44 of the Scotland Act provides for the creation of the 'Scottish Executive' which, under section 44(1)(c), includes 'the Lord Advocate and the Solicitor General for Scotland'. Section 57(2) of the same Act provides that a member of the Scottish Executive has no power to make any subordinate legislation, or to do any other act, so far as the legislation or act is 'incompatible with any of the Convention rights' (or with Community law). Section 57(3), however, provides that subsection (2) does not apply to an act of the Lord Advocate:

> '(a) in prosecuting any offence, or
>
> (b) in his capacity as head of the systems of criminal prosecution and investigation of deaths in Scotland',

which, because of section 6(2) of the Human Rights Act 1998 would not be unlawful within the meaning of section 6(1).

Section 57(3), therefore, allows the Lord Advocate to rely on the 'protection' afforded by section 6(2) of the Human Rights Act. The need for section 57(3) was explained by the Lord Advocate in the following terms during the debates on the Human Rights Bill:

> '[Section 57(3)] ensures that this protection is also afforded to the Lord Advocate where it is alleged that he has breached [section 57(2) of the Scotland Act] which requires him to act compatibly with the Convention rights. This ensures that the Lord Advocate would prosecute an offence contained in a United Kingdom Act even if it were in contravention of a right. Without the amendment of the offence could be prosecuted by the Crown Prosecution service in England but not by the Lord Advocate. The amendment also allows him to act in his capacity as head of the systems of

criminal prosecution and investigation of deaths in Scotland if he is acting as required by a provision of a United Kingdom Act.'[102]

How do sections 6(2) and 57(3) affect the issue of prosecutorial discretion in Scotland? In answering that question the following points need to be noted:

(i) Section 6(2) applies only to *statutory* obligations and powers

The first point that is worth noting is that the protection afforded by section 6(2) applies only to *statutory* obligations and powers. It does not, indeed cannot, have any application where the action taken by the public authority is taken in exercise of a common law duty or power. If the exercise of a common law duty or power is incompatible with a Convention right then there is no place for section 6(2), and hence none for section 57(3) either.

(ii) Section 6(2)(a) and the absolute discretion of the Lord Advocate

The second point is that section 6(2)(a) is unlikely to have any bearing on prosecution discretion. This is because it applies only to the case in which the public authority is *required* by primary legislation to act in a way which is incompatible with a Convention right, and our current understanding is that the Lord Advocate and his deputies are never *required* to prosecute. Therefore, section 6(2)(a) could never be invoked as a defence to a prosecution, taken under United Kingdom legislation, which was incompatible with a Convention right. The only exception would be if the legislation imposed a statutory duty to prosecute, which would be something of an innovation, to say the least.

(iii) Section 6(2)(a) applies only to Westminster legislation

The third point is that section 6(2)(a) has no application to the case of Acts of the Scottish Parliament. The reason for this is that section 6(2)(a) applies only to the case where it is claimed that the public authority is obliged by 'primary legislation' to act in a particular way, and for the purposes of the Human Rights Act 'primary legislation' does not include Acts of the Scottish Parliament.[103]

(iv) Section 6(2)(b): the permissive defence

Section 6(2)(b) may have more relevance. This provision envisages a situation in which the public authority, although not obliged to do so, is acting so as to give effect to primary legislation, or to provisions made under primary legislation. Here, there is a defence. Again, it can apply only where the legislation in question is legislation of the United Kingdom Parliament. One assumes that by invoking

---

[102] *Hansard*, HL, 28/10/98, col 2041.
[103] Human Rights Act 1998, s 21.

this subsection, the public prosecutor is raising a defence to a claim that a prosecution involves some feature which violates Convention rights. Strictly speaking, it could apply to the case where the public prosecutor has taken proceedings in the knowledge that this was the case, but one assumes that the occasion would not arise where such action was taken.

CONCLUSION

The full impact of the European Convention on Human Rights upon our criminal justice system will not really be felt until the Human Rights Act itself comes into effect on 2 October 2000. It would, furthermore, be premature and not the purpose of this chapter to even briefly examine the 'devolution issue' judgments to date of the Court of Criminal Appeal. However, it may be of some relevance and interest to the reader to note that the questions of legality and extent of prosecutorial powers have arisen already in a number of cases. One example is that of a plea in bar of trial invoking unreasonable delay in terms of Art 6 of the ECHR where it was ruled that the onus rests with the Crown to explain the delay and the accused need not demonstrate prejudice.[104] Another example is the ruling that the Crown cannot seek a remedy from the court which is not compatible with the ECHR.[105] Such decisions, and others, have simply begun to demonstrate the potential impact of ECHR rights on our system of criminal justice.

---

[104] *H M Advocate* v *Little* 1999 SCCR 625.
[105] *H M Advocate* v *Scottish Media Newspapers Ltd* 1999 SCCR 599 at 603.

7: CRIMINAL PROCEDURE, CONVENTION RIGHTS AND THE CONSEQUENCES OF INCORPORATION

Alastair Brown

INTRODUCTION

After somewhat uncertain beginnings,[1] the European Convention on the Protection of Human Rights and Fundamental Freedoms 1950 ('ECHR') has developed into what the late President of the European Court of Human Rights ('ECtHR') once called 'a regional human rights protection system of unparalleled effectiveness'.[2] But, although the United Kingdom accepted the right of individual petition under the Convention as early as 1966,[3] it has never been incorporated into UK law and its availability for use in UK courts has until now been severely limited.[4] Between them, the Human Rights Act 1998 and parts of the Scotland Act 1998 change that. It is increasingly clear that the consequences of incorporation may be far reaching indeed. This is at least as true of criminal law as it is of any other area of law.[5]

This chapter assesses the probable effect of the incorporation of the Convention rights on Scottish criminal law, paying particular attention to criminal evidence and procedure. The thesis which it advances is that, although the consequences of incorporation will be far reaching, the changes which are likely to be produced in Scottish criminal law thereby will be of an organic nature and not a disjunctive one. With few exceptions, existing principles and practices will be developed in a way which will be informed by the Convention rights and their associated jurisprudence. They will not be jettisoned and replaced with unfamiliar concepts.

The attempt to predict the effect of incorporation on Scots criminal law is, of course, attended with considerable risk. As a result of the rule in *T, Petitioner*[6] and *R v Secretary of State for the Home Department, ex parte Brind*[7] hitherto it has not, in theory, been legitimate to refer to ECHR except where a legislative provision to be

---

[1] See Geoffrey Marston, 'The United Kingdom's Part in the Preparation of the European Convention on Human Rights, 1950' (1993) 42 ICLQ 796.
[2] R Ryssdall, 'The Coming of Age of the European Convention on Human Rights' [1996] EHRLR 18.
[3] For an account of this, see Lord Lester of Herne Hill, 'UK Acceptance of the Strasbourg Jurisdiction: What Really went on in Whitehall in 1965' [1998] PL 237.
[4] For the UK Government's traditional justification of its position, see HL Debs, vol 524, cols 209–13 (5 December 1990); and Sir Nicholas Lyell, 'Whither Strasbourg? Why Britain Should Think Long and Hard Before Incorporating the European Convention on Human Rights' [1997] EHRLR 132. For the reasoning behind incorporation, see Jack Straw and Paul Boateng, 'Bringing Rights Home. Labour's Plans to Incorporate the European Convention on Human Rights into UK Law' [1997] EHRLR 71.
[5] See, for example, A T H Smith, 'The Human Rights and the Criminal Lawyer: The Constitutional Context' [1999] Crim LR 251; Andrew Ashworth, 'Article 6 and the Fairness of Trials' [1999] Crim LR 261.
[6] 1997 SLT 724, 1996 SCLR 897.
[7] [1991] AC 696, [1991] 2 WLR 588, [1991] 1 All ER 720.

interpreted was patently ambiguous. In the case of such ambiguity, ECHR could be used as an aid to interpretation.[8] However, Lord Justice-General Hope was prepared, in *Anderson v HM Advocate*,[9] to consider the case law of ECtHR, distinguishing *Brind* on the basis that in *Anderson* the High Court was not concerned with statutory interpretation, so that the need to recognise the supremacy of Parliament, which underlay the approach in *Brind*, did not arise. More recently, the Lord Justice-General has made it clear, in *McLeod, Petitioner*,[10] that the High Court will be prepared, in seeking to formulate an approach to Scots law, to look at the decisions of ECtHR for their persuasive effect in the same way as it would look at the decisions of any other court of authority. These two cases lend support to Hunt's contention that, apart from incorporation, there is actually much greater scope for the use of ECHR material in UK courts than one might have thought.[11] Nevertheless, in practice, Murdoch is right to assert that a lack of awareness of the content and possibilities of ECHR amongst Scots practitioners has led to a situation in which, for all its vaunted continental roots, Scots law has hitherto accorded ECHR a standing which is in fact weaker than that which it enjoys in any other Western European legal system.[12] Such attempts as have been made so far to invoke ECHR law in the Scottish courts have sometimes been marked by an apparent failure to understand its most basic features.[13]

Accordingly, no one has yet explored in practice the ways in which Convention law applies to the Scottish criminal law. As a result, anything said in this or any other essay about the application of the Convention rights in the Scottish criminal court is necessarily provisional. But once it is agreed that incorporation of the Convention rights will have an effect, the question 'what sort of effect?' becomes irresistible, at least to this writer; and so the risk is taken. At the very least, some of the analysis made in support of the thesis should have lasting value. It should be said, of course, that the opinions expressed and the argument made are those of the writer alone and that it should not be thought that they represent, to any extent, the views or policies of the Crown Office, the Procurator Fiscal Service or the Law Officers.

CONVENTION RIGHTS AND PARLIAMENTARY SOVEREIGNTY

The relationship between the Convention rights and Parliamentary sovereignty is explored by Professor Miller elsewhere in this volume. For that reason, it is not analysed here. It is, however, important to the argument which it is sought to make to state that it was the Government's clear policy, in enacting both the

---

[8] See F A R Bennion, *Statutory Interpretation: A Code* (3rd edn, Butterworths 1997) p 523; Andrew J Cunningham, 'The European Convention on Human Rights, Customary International Law and the Constitution' (1994) 43 ICLQ 537; William C Gilmore and Stephen C Neff, 'On Scotland, Europe and Human Rights' in Hector L MacQueen (ed), *Scots Law into the 21st Century: Essays in Honour of W A Wilson* (W Green/Sweet & Maxwell, 1996) 265.
[9] 1998 SLT 155.
[10] 1998 JC 67, 1998 SLT 233, 1998 SCCR 77.
[11] Murray Hunt, *Using Human Rights Law in English Courts* (Hart Publishing, 1998).
[12] Jim Murdoch, 'Scotland and the European Convention', in Brice Dickson (ed), *Human Rights and the European Convention*, (Sweet & Maxwell, 1997) p 113.
[13] See, for example, *Jardine v Crowe* 1999 JC 59, 1999 SCCR 52 in which the appellant's argument was founded on an entirely erroneous understanding of the relationship between ECHR and EC law.

Human Rights Act and the Scotland Act, not to interfere with the doctrine of Parliamentary sovereignty. There are limitations on the requirement to interpret legislation so that it is consistent with the Convention rights and on the rule that public authorities which act incompatibly with the Convention rights act unlawfully.

As to the first of these, the Government's expectation, when a court finds it impossible to find an interpretation of a piece of legislation which is consistent with the Convention rights, is clear. At second reading of the Human Rights Bill in the House of Lords, the Lord Chancellor said that 'the Bill does not allow the courts to set aside or ignore Acts of Parliament' and that section 3 'preserves the effect of primary legislation which is incompatible with the Convention'.[14] Later in the same debate, he said that the intention of the legislation was to maximise the protection to individuals 'while retaining the fundamental principle of Parliamentary sovereignty'.[15] The remedy provided for the situation in which a court cannot find a way to construe legislation compatibly with the Convention rights is the declaration of incompatibility, which will not affect the validity, continuing operation or enforcement of the provision in respect of which it is given and which will not bind the parties to the proceedings in which it is made.[16] Such a declaration might well prompt the Government to make legislative change but will not oblige it to do so.

As to the second, the effect of section 6 (which makes it unlawful for a public authority to act in a way which is incompatible with a Convention right) is limited by subsection (2), by which subsection (1) does not apply if the public authority concerned could not have acted differently as a result of primary legislation, or if the act challenged was carried out so as to give effect to or enforce primary legislation. Accordingly, even if it is irrefutably the case that what a police officer or prosecutor has done is incompatible with a Convention right, the act in question will not be unlawful if it was done to give effect to or enforce primary legislation. Section 57(2) of the Scotland Act, which renders acts of members of the Scottish Executive (and hence of the Lord Advocate) *ultra vires* if they are incompatible with any of the Convention rights, is qualified by subsection (3), the effect of which is to prevent acts of the Lord Advocate from being *ultra vires* if they are within the scope of section 6(2) of the Human Rights Act—that is, if the Lord Advocate was acting so as to give effect to or enforce the provisions of primary UK legislation. Accordingly, even if there is an unassailable argument to be made that the Lord Advocate has acted or proposes to act in some way incompatibly with the Convention rights that argument will avail nothing if what was done was required in terms of UK primary legislation.

It is clear that Parliament had no intention of allowing its own position to be undermined by its human rights legislation and that it intended to retain control over the future of legislative provisions found by the courts to be incompatible with the Convention rights. So far as Scottish criminal procedure is concerned, the Criminal Procedure (Scotland) Act 1995 represents a very comprehensive codification of the law. Other aspects of procedure are dealt with in statutes such as the Criminal Law (Consolidation) (Scotland) Act 1995, the Proceeds of Crime

---

[14] HL Deb, 3 November 1997, cols 1230–1231.
[15] HL Deb, 3 November 1997, col 1294.
[16] Human Rights Act 1998, s 4(6).

(Scotland) Act 1995 and the Crime and Punishment (Scotland) Act 1997. Although criminal procedure is within the legislative competence of the Scottish Parliament and legislation of that Parliament will be capable of being struck down if it is incompatible with the Convention rights,[17] the position at present and for the foreseeable future is that Scottish criminal procedure is substantially regulated by UK primary legislation. It is submitted that those steps in procedure which have the sanction of that legislation will be effectively protected from a challenge based on an averment of incompatibility with Convention rights. In consequence, one should not anticipate any fundamental changes to criminal procedure as a result of incorporation of the Convention rights. There may be successful challenges to the ways in which discretion is exercised but the human rights legislation precludes more radical departures. No doubt there will be change but it will be organic, not disjunctive.

THE HIGH COURT AND CONVENTION LAW

ECHR has hitherto been invoked relatively little in Scottish criminal courts. In those cases in which it has been considered, however, there has been a noticeable tendency for the High Court to blend Convention law and existing Scots law so as to produce a result which is not dramatically different from that which could have been achieved under reference to Scots law alone.

Anderson

We have mentioned the cases of *Anderson* and *McLeod*. In *Anderson* the point was the alleged incompetence of the defence. Lord Justice-General Hope began by demonstrating, from purely Scottish authority, that the right to a fair trial is an essential principle of Scottish criminal justice. He then analysed that right in terms of the rights to be told what accusation is made, to have sufficient notice to prepare and to have one's defence presented to the court. Those rights are, he said, 'the equivalent in Scotland of those described in Arts 6.1 and 6.3(a) to (c) of the European Convention on Human Rights'. The Convention articles were 'not part of our domestic law *but the principles which they describe have, for a long time, been established as part of the law of this country*'.[18] Lord Hope was unable to find anything of particular relevance in the Convention cases to which the Court was referred and went on to decide the case on the basis of Scots (and some English) authority.

McLeod

In *McLeod* (which was concerned with the content of the Crown's duty of disclosure), Lord Justice-General Rodger examined certain Convention authorities and decided that they did not support the approach for which the

---

[17] Scotland Act 1998, s 29(1) and (2).
[18] At p 158, (emphasis added).

appellant's counsel contended. He noted that 'counsel did not dispute that, overall, our system ensured a fair trial for accused persons' and went on immediately to say that 'it would indeed be strange if that were not the case since the plea of oppression exists to protect the accused's right to a fair trial'.[19] The Lord Justice-General then went on to explain the ways in which that right is secured by existing Scots law. The Lord Justice-Clerk (Cullen), in *his* opinion in the case pointed out that, although ECtHR and *Edwards* v *United Kingdom*[20] found the proposition that the prosecution must disclose all material evidence for or against the accused, they neither prescribe a particular method of disclosure nor require uniformity as to method as between the several states parties to ECHR. Putting it shortly, the Court held that the disclosure routinely made by the Crown, coupled with defence precognition, satisfy the Art 6(3)(b) requirement for adequate facilities for preparation.

Ucak

In *Ucak* v *HM Advocate*[21] the appellant was a Turkish Kurd who did not understand English. He was detained in connection with his possession of a large quantity of heroin and in due course interviewed in the presence of an interpreter, who was subsequently the interpreter at the trial. Sundry procedure had, however, taken place at the police station before the interpreter arrived. It was argued, on the basis of *Anderson*, that reference to ECHR was legitimate, asserted that the appellant had been unable to understand what had taken place before the arrival of the interpreter and argued that the procedure at the police station had been unfair so that the conviction should be quashed. Without specifically addressing the Convention argument, the High Court held that there was no reasonable suspicion that the appellant had not received a fair trial and declined to disturb the conviction. In his commentary on the report of the case, Sheriff Gordon suggests that ECHR could 'perhaps be regarded as virtually incorporated into Scots law already'. If he is right about this, it would follow that substantial change should not be expected.

Consequences

Since the argument in *Ucak* was made under reference to *Anderson*, in which (as we have seen) Lord Hope was careful to restrict the use of Convention law to cases which did not involve statute, and since in *T, Petitioner* Lord Hope specifically adopted the English rules which limit reference to ECHR to cases of statutory ambiguity, Sheriff Gordon probably goes too far in his comment on *Ucak*. Nevertheless, it does seem to be legitimate to assert that the High Court has already been paying significant attention to ECHR and that it has been at pains to integrate its provisions with existing Scots law. To be sure, that may simply reflect the limitations which existing law placed on the use of the Convention and which

---

[19] At p 242.
[20] (1993) 15 EHRR 417.
[21] 1998 SCCR 517.

will be removed by the Human Rights Act; but it does seem unlikely that the High Court, having asserted in *Anderson* and *McLeod* that fairness is a fundamental principle of Scots law which may be vindicated, *inter alia*, through pleas based on oppression, will depart suddenly from that position just because of the enactment of the Human Rights Act.

EXISTING CONSISTENCY

This is particularly so because, it is asserted, substantial consistency already exists between the Strasbourg case-law and Scots law. Even if parliamentary sovereignty was not preserved and even if the High Court was not already blending Convention law and Scots law, the level of agreement between Convention law and Scottish criminal procedure law is such that, whilst one might expect to see Convention law used as a most important resource for understanding and developing Scots law, one could not reasonably expect to find dramatic change rendered necessary.

The extent of the agreement between Scots law and Convention law cannot be explored comprehensively in the space available here. What we can do, however, is to examine some aspects of Articles 8, 5 and 6 as they bear on criminal procedure.

Article 8

Article 8 has been one of the most dynamically interpreted provisions of ECHR and what is said about it here deals with only a very small part of its ambit.[22] It follows a pattern common to many of the Convention rights in that it states a right and then states the circumstances in which interference with the right may be permitted. Interference must, first, be in accordance with the law. Second, it must be necessary. Third, it must be in pursuit of one of the specified objectives. In a criminal procedure context, the prevention of disorder or crime and the protection of the rights and freedoms of others are most likely to be relevant. In *Funke* v *France*,[23] ECtHR held that the exceptions provided for by Article 8(2) are to be interpreted narrowly, that the need for them in a given case must be convincingly established and that the relevant legislation and practice must afford adequate and effective safeguards against abuse. In the same case, ECtHR held that Article 8 is apt to cover search.

Granted that search is a *prima facie* interference with the private life and home of the person whose property is the subject of the search, it will be necessary to consider it against the three criteria set out in Article 8(2).

First, it must be in accordance with law. This, it is suggested, is not likely to be a problem. We have a large and well-developed body of law on search with and without warrant.[24] Assuming compliance with that law, the first criterion will be met.

---

[22] For an overview, see David Feldman, 'The Developing Scope of Article 8 of the European Convention on Human Rights' [1997] EHRLR 265.
[23] (1993) 16 EHRR 297.
[24] See generally Alastair N Brown, *Criminal Evidence and Procedure: An Introduction* (T&T Clark, 1996) p 35 *et seq*.

The third criterion is the pursuit of one of the specified objectives. Generally it will be possible to see a search as being in pursuit of the prevention of crime (a concept which has been understood quite widely by ECtHR) or for the protection of the rights and freedoms of others. Those rights and freedoms may include the Article 2 right to life (where it is drugs which are sought) and the Article 1, Protocol 1 right to property (where the police are attempting to recover stolen property). This criterion will therefore also frequently be met.

It is in the second criterion, necessity, that the interest lies. This criterion inevitably introduces issues of balance and proportionality. How serious is the crime being investigated? Is it really necessary to break in the door at three a m? For a firearms offence the answer is likely to be 'yes'. For a minor shoplifting, the answer is likely to be 'no'. Cases falling in between these extremes will have to be decided on their own facts.

It is suggested, however, that this is not actually very far from our existing law. What sheriff would grant a search warrant for a minor shoplifting where no other considerations (such as repetition of the offence) are present? What fiscal would even ask for one? If the offence is trivial, how could it be argued that urgency excuses search without warrant? It is suggested that Article 8 offers a new framework within which to reason but that the outcome might very well not differ markedly from what would happen already. In one particular respect, it is suggested, it would not differ at all. If there is a breach of Article 8, it will make the search irregular; but that does not make the results of the search inevitably inadmissible. In *Chinoy* v *United Kingdom*,[25] the Commission was prepared to accept that there might well be occasions when irregularly (or, in that case, unlawfully) obtained evidence might be admitted. ECtHR took a similar view in *Schenk* v *Switzerland*.[26] Ashworth maintains (correctly, it is submitted) that *Schenk* 'confirms that there is no automatic rule of exclusion to be deduced from Article 6(1), but it leaves open the question whether the exclusory discretion is exercised properly in a given case'.[27] Existing domestic law tells us that irregularities may be excused.[28] *Chinoy* and *Schenk* tell us that Convention law contemplates that possibility as well.

Article 5

Article 5 deals with the detention of the accused. Article 5(1) follows the pattern of stating the right and then stating the permitted exceptions. Subparagraphs (a) to (e) state those exceptions exhaustively and fall to be construed narrowly.[29] It has been said that Article 5's 'principal aim is to prevent arbitrary deprivation of liberty. The emphasis is on procedural rights, with little scope for challenging the merits of decisions on deprivation of liberty'.[30]

At the time of writing there is talk of challenges being made to the compatibility

---

[25] Application No 15199/89, 4 September 1991.
[26] (1991) 13 EHRR 242.
[27] Op cit, note 5 above, p 270.
[28] *Lawrie* v *Muir* 1950 JC 19, 1950 SLT 37.
[29] *Winterwerp* v *Netherlands* (1979–80) 2 EHRR 387.
[30] Karen Reid, *A Practitioner's Guide to the European Convention on Human Rights* (Sweet & Maxwell, 1998) p 178.

of section 14 of the Criminal Procedure (Scotland) Act 1995 with the Convention rights and in particular with Article 5(1)(c). The argument seems to proceed on the basis that Article 5(1)(c) only authorises arrest or detention for the purpose of bringing the person concerned before the competent legal authority (i e the court), but that section 14 does not necessarily result in the placing of the detained person before the court; he might, instead, be liberated. But in *Brogan* v *United Kingdom*[31] ECtHR said that Article 5(1)(c) 'does not presuppose that the police should have obtained sufficient evidence to bring charges' and proceeded on the basis that it is legitimate to detain so as to further an investigation and that, if sufficient evidence was obtained during that investigation, no doubt the person detained would be put before the court. In *Brogan* the persons detained were not in fact placed before the court (because there was insufficient evidence after investigation). ECtHR did not find a breach of the Convention in that regard.[32] It does not seem possible to say, then, that section 14 detention is not sanctioned by Article 5(1)(c).

Article 5(3) entitles the accused to trial within a reasonable time or to release pending trial. It is clear that, in Convention terms, if the accused is to be kept in custody there must be relevant and sufficient grounds for doing so. Reid suggests that, for a short period (by which she means a 'matter of months'), suspicion itself suffices for keeping the accused in custody[33]; though in *Tomasi* v *France*[34] it was held that suspicion alone was not enough to justify a remand in custody which lasted over five years. No exhaustive list of other reasons justifying the remand of the accused in custody exists. The principle was stated by ECtHR in *Letellier* v *France*[35] to be that the court before which the accused is brought must consider 'all the facts arguing for and against the existence of a genuine requirement of public interest' for the remanding of the accused in custody. In *CC* v *United Kingdom*[36] the Commission said that 'the judge must examine all the facts arguing for and against the existence of a genuine requirement of public interest justifying, with due regard to the presumption of innocence, a departure from the rule of respect for the accused's liberty'.

Some commentators have classified the Strasbourg cases in four categories: prevention of crime, danger of flight, risk of interference with the course of justice and prevention of public disorder. This categorisation is, however, no more than an analytical tool. As to the prevention of crime, it was held in *Toth* v *Austria*[37] that previous convictions could be relied on as giving reasonable grounds to fear that further offences would be committed. The danger of flight will vary according to the strength of the accused's ties with the jurisdiction and the court should consider financial guarantees (which include, but are not limited to, money bail) as a means of offsetting the risk.[38] The risk of interference with the course of justice requires to be kept under review and, if it disappears, liberation should follow unless there are other grounds for keeping the accused in custody.[39] Finally, the

---

[31] (1989) 11 EHRR 117.
[32] There was held to have been a breach in *Brogan* but that was on the separate basis that detention had lasted for over four days, which was too long.
[33] Reid, op cit, note 30 above, p 307.
[34] (1993) 15 EHRR 1.
[35] (1992) 14 EHRR 83.
[36] [1999] Crim LR 228.
[37] (1992) 14 EHRR 551.
[38] *Letellier* above; *Matznetter* v *Austria* (1979–80) 1 EHRR 198.
[39] *Kemmache No 1* v *France* (1992) 14 EHRR 520.

cases on prevention of public disorder have related to terrorist offences[40] or the exceptional circumstances of a high-profile, premeditated murder.[41]

The grounds on which bail may be refused in Scots law are set out most clearly in *Smith v McCallum*[42] in which the Lord Justice-Clerk (Wheatley) said that where an accused has a criminal record which, together with the present charges, raises the question of the protection of the public, or is in some sense in a position of trust in relation to the court (eg on probation, deferred sentence or community service), unless there are cogent reasons for deciding otherwise, bail should be refused. Other grounds of refusal are the nature of the offence, intimidation of witnesses, no fixed abode and reasonable grounds to suspect the accused will fail to appear. This approach is not nowadays applied as rigorously as it was in the days when Lord Wheatley wrote personal letters remonstrating with any sheriff who granted bail in circumstances in which the *McCallum* judgment should have precluded it; and that very softening of the approach seems likely to avoid difficulties associated with absolute prohibitions on bail. More generally, it is suggested, there is relatively little difference between the *McCallum* approach and that taken by ECtHR.

Article 5(4) entitles the accused to take proceedings by which the lawfulness of his detention shall be decided. This is a different issue from the *appropriateness* of a remand in custody, which is dealt with under Article 5(3). Under Article 5(4) it is the *lawfulness* of the detention which is in issue. It seems clear that, while Scots law contemplates committal for further examination on petition on the basis of something less than a sufficiency of evidence[43] (which must mean reasonable suspicion), full committal on petition will only be lawful if there is a sufficiency of evidence.[44] It is accepted by the Crown that the same test applies where an accused is detained in custody pending trial on a summary complaint. It follows from Article 5(4) that the accused must be placed in a position to dispute the lawfulness of the detention and that means that he must be placed in a position to dispute the Crown's (hitherto implied) contention that it has a sufficiency of evidence.

If the accused is given no information about the evidence which the Crown has, he cannot meaningfully bring under review the lawfulness of the detention and Article 5(4) cannot be satisfied. In *Lamy v Belgium*[45] it was held that the principle of equality of arms applies to Article 5(4) so that the accused must be afforded the opportunity to present his case under conditions which do not place him at a substantial disadvantage vis-à-vis the Crown.[46]

The Crown has taken the view that the option of doing nothing about this is not open; but nothing in either Convention case-law or Scots law would justify an attempt to investigate the merits of the case at this early stage; that is a matter properly reserved for the trial. It does seem that the accused should be in a position to debate the sufficiency of the Crown case on paper at full committal

---

[40] Eg *Tomasi* above.
[41] *Letellier* above.
[42] 1982 SLT 421, 1982 SCCR 115.
[43] *Alison*, ii p 134; *Macdonald* (5th edn) p 203.
[44] *Macdonald* (5th edn) p 204; *Alison* ii, p 137; *Adair v McGarry* 1933 JC 72, 1933 SLT 482 at p 487 per LJ-C (Alness); *Currie v McGlennan* 1989 SLT 872 at p 873 per LJ-C (Ross).
[45] (1989) 11 EHRR 529.
[46] *Dombo Beheer BV v Netherlands* (1994) 18 EHRR 213.

and, in order to place him in a position to do so, the Crown has begun to provide the custody statement—a written summary of the evidential basis of its case. It is therefore open to the accused to debate the Crown's contention that the summary discloses a paper sufficiency but not to attempt to open up the issue of the reliability of the information in the Crown's possession, since that is a matter for trial.

Article 6

Article 6 entitles the accused, in the determination of the charge, to a fair hearing. We shall look shortly at selected specific guarantees but there is one more general point to be made first.

It would be entirely incorrect to understand Article 6 as conferring absolute rights on the accused. Unlike Article 8, for example, it does not on its face demand a balancing exercise. ECtHR, however, addressed that whole issue in *Doorson* v *The Netherlands*.[47] The case concerned the use of anonymous witnesses and its facts do not concern us here. However, in the course of its judgment, ECtHR said this[48]:

> 'It is true that Article 6 does not explicitly require the interests of witnesses in general, and those of victims called upon to testify in particular, to be taken into consideration. However, their life, liberty or security of person may be at stake, as may interests coming generally within the ambit of Article 8 of the Convention. Such interests of witnesses and victims are in principle protected by other, substantive provisions of the Convention, which imply that Contracting States should organise their criminal proceedings in such a way that those interests are not unjustifiably imperilled. Against this background, principles of fair trial also require that in appropriate cases the interests of the defence are balanced against those of witnesses and victims called upon to testify.'

This may be seen in the context of ECtHR's earlier remark in *Soering* v *United Kingdom*[49] that 'inherent in the whole of the Convention is a search for a fair balance between the demands of the general interest of the community and the requirements of the protection of the individual's fundamental rights' (a remark made in the context of Article 3 of ECHR, which might well be the most absolute of the Convention rights).

We should now think back to some basic authorities in Scots law. In *Miln* v *Cullen*,[50] Lord Wheatley said (in the context of a debate about the admissibility of evidence) that

> '. . . it is the function of the court to seek to provide a proper balance to secure that the rights of individuals are properly preserved, while not hamstringing the police in their investigation of crime with a series of

---

[47] (1996) 22 EHRR 330.
[48] Judgment, para 70.
[49] (1989) 11 EHRR 439, Judgment, para 89.
[50] 1967 JC 21, 1967 SLT 35.

academic vetoes which ignore the realities and practicalities of the situation and discount completely the public interest'.

And in *Skeen v McLaren*,[51] where the Crown sought to have a summary trial adjourned because witnesses were not available, Lord Justice-General Emslie said:

> 'When a motion is made by one party or the other to adjourn a diet of this kind on this ground and no question arises as to whether it is well founded in fact, there are two questions to which the sheriff must address his mind if he is to arrive at a proper decision upon the motion. The first question is whether the grant or refusal of the motion will be prejudicial to the accused and if so what is the probable extent of that prejudice. The second question is whether prejudice to the prosecutor would result from the granting or refusal of the motion and once again the degree of probable prejudice must be estimated ... To these two questions we would add a possible third, namely prejudice to the public interest which may arise independently of prejudice to the accused or to the prosecution in the particular case in which the motion is made.'

It is suggested that what the High Court said in these two cases expresses the same principle as was expressed by ECtHR in *Doorson* and *Soering*. A proper process of justice takes into account not only the interests of the accused, not only the interests of the victim, not only the interests of the witnesses, not only the interests of the public but *all* of those interests. It will seek to balance the various interests engaged and the weight which each of them will bear will vary according to the circumstances of each case. This, it is suggested, is what the Scottish courts have been accustomed to doing in any event, and so the point supports the thesis advanced in this paper. As Sharpe has demonstrated, ECHR is not a suspect's charter[52]; but neither is it a victim's charter. It is both.

There are two particular guarantees under Article 6 which require attention here. The first is the presumption of innocence, guaranteed by Article 6(2); and the second is Article 6(3)(d) and its application to hearsay.

In *Barberà, Messegué and Jabardo v Spain*,[53] ECtHR said that

> 'Paragraph 2 [of Article 6] embodies the principle of the presumption of innocence. It requires, *inter alia*, that when carrying out their duties the members of a court should not start with the preconceived idea that the accused has committed the offence charged, and any doubt should benefit the accused.'

This, it is suggested, fits perfectly with our existing understanding of the presumption. It would be difficult to improve on Lord Sankey LC's formulation of this in *Woolmington v DPP*[54] an English case but one which expresses the Scottish principle equally well:

---

[51] 1976 SLT (Notes) 14.
[52] See Sybil Sharpe, 'The European Convention: A Suspect's Charter?' [1997] Crim LR 848.
[53] (1989) 11 EHRR 360.
[54] [1935] AC 462.

> '... it is the duty of the prosecution to prove the prisoner's guilt ... If at the end of and on the whole of the case, there is a reasonable doubt, created by the evidence given by either the prosecution or the prisoner ... the prosecution has not made out the case and the prisoner is entitled to an acquittal. No matter what the charge or where the trial, the principle that the prosecution must prove the guilt of the prisoner is part of the common law ... and no attempt to whittle it down can be entertained.'

Thus far, the Article 6(2) jurisprudence supports the thesis that change will not be disjunctive.

From Article 6(2), ECtHR has derived the principle of the right to silence[55] but it held in *Murray v United Kingdom*[56] that the right is not absolute. In that case the evidence against the applicant had been formidable. ECtHR said that

> 'on the one hand it is self evident that it is incompatible with the immunities under consideration to base a conviction solely or mainly on the accused's silence or on a refusal to answer questions or to give evidence himself. On the other hand, the Court deems it equally obvious that these immunities cannot and should not prevent that the accused's silence, in situations which clearly call for an explanation from him, be taken into account in assessing the persuasiveness of evidence adduced by the prosecution.'

It seems, on the basis of this, that the more limited use which Scots law permits the prosecutor to make of the accused's silence at judicial examination or trial would probably be within the limits permitted by Article 6(2).

ECtHR has also addressed presumptions under the heading of Article 6(2). In *Salabiaku v France*[57] it said that:

> 'presumptions of fact or of law operate in every legal system. Clearly the Convention does not prohibit such presumptions in principle. It does, however, require the Contracting States to remain within certain limits in this respect as regards criminal law ... It requires States to confine them within reasonable limits which take into account the importance of what is at stake and maintain the rights of the defence.'

The critical issue is whether there is a facility for rebutting the presumption in question; and it is suggested that Scots law makes presumptions rebuttable, so that it is in this respect consistent with the Convention rights.

We turn, finally, to Article 6(3)(d) and hearsay. Hearsay evidence in Scotland is dealt with under section 259 of the Criminal Procedure (Scotland) Act 1995 and owes its origins to the Scottish Law Commission Report 'Evidence: Report on Hearsay Evidence in Criminal Proceedings'.[58] It is not intended to describe that law in detail here—or indeed at all—it is assumed that it is familiar. What is important is the fact that the Law Commission consciously and deliberately set

---

[55] *Saunders v United Kingdom* (1997) 23 EHRR 313.
[56] (1996) 22 EHRR 29.
[57] (1991) 13 EHRR 379.
[58] Scot Law Com No 149, 1995.

out to ensure that what they recommended was compatible with ECHR. The Convention law is as follows.

Article 6(3)(d) provides, so far as relevant, that the accused is entitled to 'have examined the witnesses against him'. The UK lawyer would read that and take the view that hearsay is absolutely excluded. Support for that position would be derived from a superficial reading of *Unterpertinger v Austria*[59] in which the applicant had been accused of assault upon his wife and stepdaughter. They had made statements to the police but declined to give evidence. He was convicted on the basis of the statements given to the police. ECtHR delivered a short judgment. The starting point was that

> 'the reading out of statements in this way cannot be regarded as being inconsistent with Article 6(1) and (3)(d) of the Convention, but the use made of them as evidence must nevertheless comply with the rights of the defence, which it is the object and purpose of Article 6 to protect. This is especially so where the person "charged with a criminal offence", who has the right under Article 6(3)(d) to "examine or have examined" witnesses against him, has not had an opportunity at any stage in the earlier proceedings to question the persons whose statements are read out at the hearing.'

The conviction had been based 'mainly' on the statements made by the wife and stepdaughter, which the Austrian court had treated as proof of the truth of the accusations rather than merely as what ECtHR referred to as 'information'. In these circumstances, ECtHR held, the applicant's defence rights had been 'appreciably restricted' so that he had not had a fair trial. The Court held that there had been a breach of Article 6(1) taken with 'the principles inherent in paragraph (3)(d)'; but it is significant that ECtHR said that the reading out of statements was not in itself inconsistent with the Convention.

The Court went further in *Asch v Austria*,[60] holding that there had been no breach where the conviction was based in part upon the statement given to the police by the complainer in the case, who was the applicant's cohabitee and who had refused to give evidence at trial. However, it was of importance in that case that the evidence of the cohabitee was not the only evidence in the case. The police had observed injuries to the complainer and there was, in addition, medical evidence (though it does not seem to have addressed the identity of the assailant). It was also of importance that the applicant, when interviewed, had given several conflicting accounts of how the complainer came by her injuries which, ECtHR said, 'tended to undermine his credibility'.

Obviously, one could not base a decision about the admissibility of Crown evidence on the credibility or otherwise of the accused. The fact that this was a relevant consideration for ECtHR simply emphasises that cases such as *Asch* are not about admissibility at all. The question is whether the trial was fair and that question has been answered with the benefit of 20/20 hindsight. If the Article 6 jurisprudence is to be used to argue that evidence should not be admitted, the argument will have to be not only that the particular evidence involves such incompatibility with a Convention right that it should not be excused but also that

---

[59] (1991) 13 EHRR 175.
[60] (1993) 15 EHRR 597.

the breach is so gross that it is possible to say, even before the trial is completed, that the trial could not possibly be fair if the evidence was admitted. This will, of course, be very difficult to do.

CONCLUSION

The thesis advanced here is that such changes as will be brought about in Scots law by incorporation will be organic rather than disjunctive; and it is suggested that this thesis has been made out, at least in theory. Whether it will prove to be so in practice will depend on the High Court. It has, however, been demonstrated that in relation to all of the aspects of the Convention rights which have been examined there exists substantial consistency between Scots law and Convention law. Even the innovation of the custody statement reflects not merely Convention law but the existing requirement of Scots law that full committal should not take place in the absence of a *prima facie* case. It should be recalled that in times past the whole Crown precognition was scrutinised by the sheriff at full committal. The submission of the evidential basis of the Crown's case to the scrutiny of the judge who is asked to remand the accused in custody is not, therefore, an entirely novel development but something of a return to our roots.

That consistency will certainly militate against disjunctive change. Other factors will do so as well. We have seen that Parliament has legislated so that action which gives effect to primary legislation cannot be attacked for incompatibility with Convention rights. In the few cases with which it has dealt involving Convention points, the High Court seems to have experienced no difficulty in interpreting Convention law and Scots law consistently with each other and there is no reason to anticipate fundamental change in that approach. After all, that which was fair before 20 May 1999 does not have its essential character changed simply by virtue of the entry into force of section 57 of the Scotland Act. Fairness is a concept which transcends treaties and legislation. ECtHR has only the jurisdiction which has been delegated to it by the States Parties under the Convention. It has not been set up with a roving commission to investigate and condemn as human rights abuses all of those practices about which its judges might individually be concerned. The Convention was drafted under reference to existing national laws and UK law contributed to a very major extent to that drafting process.[61] It would be simply unrealistic to imagine that it would be necessary to tear up our existing law and start again.

That having been said, Scots criminal lawyers have a reputation (whether deserved or not) for being parochial. Farmer has pointed out that 'Scottish criminal law has been shaped by its determination to remain independent from its English neighbour', that this determination is particularly evident in criminal matters and that

> 'much of the writing on Scots criminal law either assumes or celebrates this difference. It may be expressed in the crude belief that Scottish law is better than English law, or, more usually, in an unreflective separatism that assumes that being Scottish, and a subject of the Scottish legal system, confers

---

[61] Marston, op cit, note 1 above.

certain benefits and that this should not be tampered with or criticised for fear of endangering a hard-won independence'.[62]

It is simply folly to believe that we have nothing to learn from other peoples' laws and from the deliberations of international human rights tribunals. Incorporation of the Convention rights is to be welcomed as a breath of fresh air in our law. Coming as it does at the time when Scots law is newly served by a dedicated Parliament, it helps to provide the conditions for a revitalisation of our criminal law in the interests of the community as a whole.

Postscript

The foregoing chapter was written before the High Court had considered cases based on section 57(2) of the Scotland Act 1998. It is now possible to say that the High Court considers the protection provided by Article 6 as similar to that provided by the plea of oppression (*Montgomery and Coulter* v *HM Advocate*, 16 November 1999) and that the application of Convention rights will take into account the Court's general knowledge of the Scottish criminal justice system (*HM Advocate* v *McGlinchey and Renicks*, 18 February 2000). While the composition of the courts has been affected significantly (*Starrs* v *Ruxton* 2000 SLT 42) there does seem to be reason to think that the chapter's prediction of organic but not disjunctive change is proving to be correct.

---

[62] L Farmer, *Criminal Law, Tradition and Legal Order: Crime and the Genius of Scots Law, 1747 to the Present* (Cambridge University Press, 1997) p 21.